# Some Call It Autumn

## *Scripture Reflections of Belief and Grace*

**James R. Welter**

Foreword by Rev. Dr. Audrey Borschel
Associate Minister, Disciples Of Christ

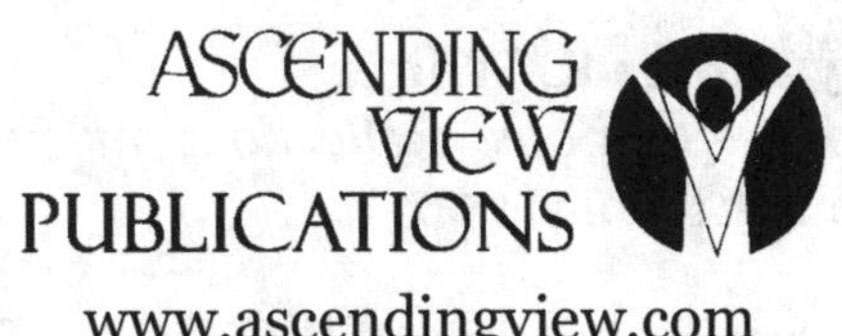


www.ascendingview.com

The ESV is an "essentially literal" translation which attempts to make the original biblical languages as transparent as possible to the reader. It gives the reader the best view of the original wording of the biblical writers. The starting point for the ESV was the 1971 Revised Standard Version (RSV). More than 90 percent of the RSV is retained in the ESV. The RSV was regarded by many as the best modern translation in terms of precision and literary elegance.

Layout and Cover Design by Mark A. Welter
Edited by James R. Welter II
Discussion Questions by Helen F. Welter

Cover Photo: “Lakeside Church in Autumn”
© PhotoLibrary / Fotosearch.com Stock Photography

ISBN: 978-0-615-69841-0

Printed in the United States of America
By United Graphics Inc.
Mattoon, IL

**Other Books by James R. Welter**

*Come Next Spring—Scripture Reflections of Promise and Hope*
Ascending View Publications, 2007

*When Winter Comes—Scripture Reflections for Daily Living*
Ascending View Publications, 2003

# Dedication

**To My Two Sons:**

***James R. Welter II, MA, University of Connecticut***
***Mark A. Welter, BA, Purdue University***

It is one of the greatest blessings of my life to have worked with my two sons, Jim and Mark, on the three books we have published: *When Winter Comes: Scripture Reflections for Daily Living, Come Next Spring: Scripture Reflections of Promise and Hope,* and now, *Some Call it Autumn: Scripture Reflections of Belief and Grace.*

I know it is natural and expected of me as their father to praise their talents and contributions – but I am in a rare position to evaluate their gifts and abilities not just as their father, but as a fellow student. I entered Indiana University as a 53-year old freshman while Mark was a sophomore at Purdue University in Lafayette, Indiana, and Jim was a senior at Ball State University in Muncie, Indiana. So I can say (almost) without prejudice, "I went to college with these guys – and they're really good at what they do!"

It seems so trite to say that I could not have done it without them, but no other words will suffice. It was my intention to include their names on the cover of this book, as a way of fully acknowledging their contributions to our publishing venture... but they told me that "it's not done that way" – and so, once again, I bowed to their professional advice.

***Jim:*** Thank you for your countless hours of editing, changing, rewriting, expanding, reworking, clarifying, and otherwise illuminating my thoughts in this book. Almost without exception, you were right – that really *was* what I meant to say! I often felt that you took a little too much pleasure in correcting "the old man," but the final revenge is mine – the pride of a father who can say of his son: "He's better at this than I am!"

***Mark:*** Thank you for your many layout ideas and creative covers, as well as your assistance in editing this, our third and final book. Your covers and appealing layout have been critical in putting our work in the hands of readers; only then is it possible for us to touch hearts and change lives. Your contributions have made all of our works more appealing and readable, and I know that many have selected our books because of the work you have done. Thanks also for the design and ongoing maintenance of our website, which makes our books accessible to people all over the world. And thanks, too, for just being a "home-town boy" and staying close to us. The opportunity to do father-son-and-grandson things together has been one of the greatest joys of my life.

"See the square stars and the purple ones that spell out your name," the little girl in daycare said to her playmate. "I never heard of a square or purple star," her friend replied. "Of course not," she said. "They never tell you about the important stuff!"

My dear sons: *this is the important stuff!* We have put on the printed page every story from my life worth telling, and viewed them through the lens of God's word. In these pages, I've set before you my most personal thoughts and beliefs. I've shared where I've come from and where I've been; I've shared with you my feelings, my failings, and my regrets.

The regrets I have about my life, and the things I would do differently as a father and a husband, haunt me still. I emerged from my childhood with many survival skills that served us well financially over the years, but because of the isolation I experienced as a child, the only "relationship tool" I possessed as you were growing up, was a hammer – and so every problem became a nail.

So I *hammered* when I should have hugged. I *hammered* when I should have listened. I *hammered* when I should have shared. And when I should have been there supporting you during the difficult times of your formative years – *I hammered.*

My deepest longing is that I could go back to the beginning and do it over – I would be so much better at it this time! I would un-say harsh words and un-do hurtful things. I would take back all of those extra hours I spent at the office, and spend them with you instead. I would un-waste the anxious days I spent on so many transient things, and I would make those years more sensitive and loving.

But I can't undo the past. I cannot change my yesterdays; life does not allow that. I can't change the beginning... all I can do is start where I am, and change the ending. And after you have looked inside the cup of your soul and dealt with *your* beginnings, I hope that the relationships we have built and the experiences we have shared in writing these books will in some way change the ending.

Through it all, I hope you can believe that – as much as I was able – I have always loved you, my two sons.

# Foreword

Over many years, I've benefitted from Jim Welter's spiritual insights on numerous biblical passages, so I was very pleased to be invited to write this foreword to Jim's third book, *Some Call it Autumn: Scripture Reflections of Belief and Grace.*

This book explores an area of faith that is often difficult to understand: the concept of grace in our lives. In a sense, we cannot define grace – but we can make each other aware of it in our midst. We tend to teach about grace by talking about God. However, Jim suggests that we may better understand the depth of grace by discovering it in our experiences, in our loving relationships, in our successes and failures – all of which are places where God speaks to us through everyday words and events.

Jim has a gift for relating scripture to our everyday lives as he shares his many personal stories – some of which are joyful, and some of which reveal grief and disappointments. All of his reflections are clear, sensitive, and often humorous, having emerged out of his lifetime of experience as a pastoral minister, public speaker, writer, scholar, and businessman.

Jim's book seeks to help us understand how grace works in our lives, and he is hopeful that you will grow in your understanding as you read his personal reflections. Perhaps you will be gently led to reflect on your own stories and, in so doing, you too will experience grace – God's greatest gift.

Yours in Christ,

Audrey Borschel

Rev. Dr. Audrey Borschel, DMin, DMA
Associate Minister, Disciples Net Church

# Introduction

Those of you who are familiar with my two previous books, *When Winter Comes* and *Come Next Spring*, may notice a difference in this work. In my first book, I related my experiences growing up on the farm and in my later parish work, and explored their connection to the words of scripture. (Unfortunately, *When Winter Comes* is now out of print, so I have incorporated some of the most popular reflections from that work into this new volume.)

In my second book, *Come Next Spring,* I attempted to address the most challenging questions of Christian life: why bad things happen to good people, why we experience grief and loss, why some prayers are not answered, and many other difficult topics. In doing so, I also expressed everything of significance that I believe about God – mainly, that God loves us, and is with us even in our times of trial and suffering.

My purpose in writing *Some Call It Autumn* is to attempt to further reveal God's grace and show how it can transform our lives. A writing professor once counseled me, "Don't tell them what you believe – tell them how you got there." Thus, the reflections in this book are longer and more personal than those in previous volumes – because this book is about *my* journey, my personal experience of God's grace at work in my life. I hope that, by sharing my journey, you may become more aware of the presence of God's grace in your own life.

I procrastinated for some time before beginning this book, and it was very difficult for me to write. For one thing, it is my third volume and will very likely be my last. That thought alone conjures up a sense of finality that one tends to avoid! And that sense of finality, of last things, brings its own uncertainties: with this last opportunity to share my spiritual journey in print, what shall I say? Which experiences should I share? What words will touch the most hearts? And, most difficult of all, how can I best express the blessing of God's saving grace?

But as I attempted to write about God's grace, I found myself in considerable discomfort and consternation. Any hope to reveal God's grace even in a limited way requires a level of emotional vulnerability that is far beyond my comfort zone. And yet, as uncomfortable as I am letting friends, family, and strangers see into my soul, I know of no other way to express the depth, wonder, and power of God's abundant grace. It therefore requires that I share thoughts and experiences that are normally reserved for a spouse, a good friend, a counselor – or perhaps a confessor.

But I cannot adequately express God's gift of grace without revealing where I've been! And one cannot truly experience God's grace without living the changes and experiencing the "letting go" that is made manifest in the dying leaves we see during the Fall season. So, unless I allow myself to be vulnerable, how can I even begin to express the transforming power of God's grace – which is so beautifully present in the season that some call Autumn?

In the 1950s, when I was growing up, life in rural Indiana was simple. We ate three meals a day: breakfast, dinner, and supper. And there were four seasons in our year: Spring, Summer, Fall, and Winter. My family usually had little money; our small farm didn't even offer the conveniences that most other poor families enjoyed, such as electricity, a telephone, a means of transportation, or indoor plumbing. And it was more than a mile to our nearest neighbor, so we were fairly isolated.

Given our situation, travel or family vacations were out of the question; as a child, these were virtually foreign concepts to me. And I always dreaded returning to school in the Fall because one of the first assignments always seemed to be, "Share with the class something you did on your summer vacation!" I was an "A" student, so being kept in at recess for not completing that assignment one year was hurtful and demeaning to me. "I don't know what she means," I protested to my friend. "All we did during the summer was take care of the garden, pick berries, work in the fields, and help with canning to get ready for next winter!" "*Everyone* goes on vacation," my third-grade teacher insisted. So I finally made up a vacation story and was once again allowed to join the other kids at recess.

As far back as I can remember, my sister Fran was my confidant. (In later years, she would teach me that striped ties and checkered shirts didn't match, and she would counsel me on how to talk to girls, as well as many of the other finer points of life that one would normally learn about from a father or an older brother.)

"That big girl in my class takes a lot of trips," I said to Fran, as I cried about the lie I had told. "But she's not so smart – she calls supper 'dinner!' And she says that 'Autumn' comes before Winter! Doesn't she know about Fall? What's 'Autumn'?" My tears became a sniffle. Fran explained: "We call the season Fall, but some people call it Autumn." "Well, that's silly," I scoffed. "Leaves *fall* to the ground, and we rake them up – they don't 'autumn' to the ground!" And Fran answered, "Autumn refers to the beauty of the season, not the work we do."

***Some call it Autumn!*** Fran's simple statement resonates with me as I live out the "autumn" of my life, with all of its uncertainties, transformations, and opportunities for growth. And as I walk this journey, grace comes as a gentle breeze flowing amongst the Autumn leaves, adding new colors to my life and beckoning me to enter this season with appreciation and joy.

I will leave it to others to try to define exactly what grace is, and I am content to let theologians argue whether it is "infused" or "imputed." My highest aspiration is simply that this book will lead you to reflect on your own life and to *experience* God's free gift of grace, which is always there and only requires our awareness and openness to it.

As you walk your own Autumn journey – whenever that may be – I hope you can let go of those things that weigh you down and let them fall to the ground like leaves. I hope that, by journey's end, you will know the peace of simply believing his word and trusting in his grace.

My prayer for you is that, as Fall approaches, his grace will enable you to see why "some call it Autumn"!

Jim Welter

Jim Welter

# Table of Contents

# Acknowledgements

**My Wife: Helen A. (Fritz) Welter, RN, CHPN**
Thank you for your unwavering support of my work and for writing the discussion questions for *Some Call It Autumn.* Your ability to ask the questions that get to the heart of the gospel will provide a challenging opportunity for spiritual growth.

**My Two Sons: James R. Welter II and Mark A. Welter**, to whom this book is dedicated.

**My Good Friend: William Bradbury**
Thank you for accepting my invitation in 2002 to write for the St. Monica e-mail reflection ministry, and thank you for administering the program for so many years.

**My Grandson: Calvin Joseph Welter**
You are the joy of our Autumn years. We love you with 'agape' love which is without any expectations or conditions. You are what we are all called to be – God's love made visible.

**The thousands of subscribers to the St. Monica Parish e-mail ministry:**
Your affirmation of my scripture reflections and your acceptance of my other two books, ***When Winter Comes,*** and ***Come Next Spring,*** have inspired this final work, ***Some Call It Autumn***.

## *The First Chapter:*

# Amazing Grace

**_Autumn Leaves_** **_Luke 13:18-21_**

*He said therefore, "What is the kingdom of God like? And to what shall I compare it? It is like a grain of mustard seed that a man took and sowed in his garden, and it grew and became a tree, and the birds of the air made nests in its branches." And again he said, "To what shall I compare the kingdom of God? It is like leaven that a woman took and hid in three measures of flour, until it was all leavened."*

Jesus' question in the above scripture passage – "To what shall I compare it?" – prompts me to ask the same question of myself: to what do *I* compare the kingdom of God?

The kingdom of God is like a day in Autumn, when the beauty of the leaves bursts forth in their dying. So it is, in dying to ourselves, that the beauty of the kingdom within *us* bursts forth.

Autumn is the season of vulnerability, in which the great arms of oak trees stretch their summer leaves upon the cool winds. All that has been alive and green is stripped from them, and the tall, wide branches seem wounded unto death. Across the lawns in layers lie the near-dead leaves; to the ground they fall, as if to say "It is over – all is lost."

This is the season when trees open wide to wounding, when the security of summer gives way to another season. The trees are wiser than we humans – we who clutch small arms around ourselves, shielding our fragile hearts, and stifling any new springtime! We have much to learn from the Autumn trees; none of us wants to be so vulnerable to winter as the trees are in Autumn. Yet our relationships and experiences of life ask us to be open – to be willing let go, so that new growth can come... and the beauty of the kingdom within us may be seen.

New growth means change! The trees tell us this! Life tells us this! *Jesus tells us this!* Every time Jesus opened himself to others – every time he reached out, every time he touched or received from others – he allowed himself to be vulnerable. When Jesus said, "You must lose your life so you may find it," he was talking about the "Autumns" of our lives. He was talking about those moments of vulnerability, when we are asked to shed our armor and to risk our relationships. He was talking about those times when we open ourselves to something new... when we surrender ourselves to God and allow his Spirit to move within and through our being... so that more of our blessings can be shared, and the beauty of the kingdom may be seen within us.

Have you ever noticed that some trees still have leaves hanging on to them, even in December? Long after Autumn is gone, some dead brown leaves still cling to certain branches. They must know that winter eventually claims them all. But, like those leaves, we sometimes think that growth is possible without letting go. Yet letting go – being vulnerable and accepting the death that is necessary for new life – is our journey into the kingdom.

*And so,*
*I ask forgiveness, God of my journey,*
*for holding on too tightly*
*for refusing to be open to new life*
*for fighting off the dying that's essential for growing*
*for insisting that I must always be secure and serene*
*for ignoring your voice when you urged me to let go*
*for doubting my inner beauty and strength*
*for resisting the truth of my journey to the kingdom*
*for not believing that the beauty of your kingdom lies within me.*

*("God of My Journey" is adapted from the poetry of an anonymous nun in Evansville, IN).*

Amazing Grace how sweet the sound
That saved and set me free
I once was lost but now I'm found
Was blind but now I see

My chains are gone
I have been set free
My God my Savior
Has rescued me

And like a flood
His mercy rains
Unending love
Amazing Grace.

*Amazing Grace*
*(My Chains are Gone)*
*Words by Chris Tomlin, 2006*

*I cannot adequately express my experience of God's grace in my life without first sharing with you who I am and where I've been. So I have chosen to begin this book by sharing my faith journey as told to my St. Monica "Christ Renews His Parish" retreat brothers in October, 1999.*

**I** was 29 years old before I first began to *suspect* that God loved me – and I was 35 years old before I became convinced of it!

That may seem a strange admission for a "cradle Catholic" like myself to make – but to appreciate my story, one must have some feeling of what it was like to be a Catholic in the 1950s. That was the era of the "Baltimore Catechism" in Catholic circles; it was an era of easy answers that were clearly expressed in black and white. Everything you needed to know about living a good life was contained in the Baltimore Catechism, and was presented in a convenient question-and-answer format. As children, we were expected to memorize the answers to those questions. On some level, the system must have worked – because, even after more than sixty years, I can still recite the answers as if Sister Gabriel had just called on me in class.

***Question:*** How many Gods are there?
***Answer:*** There is one God in three divine persons, Father, Son and Holy Ghost.

***Question:*** Why did God make you?
***Answer:*** God made me to know him, to love him, and to serve him in this life, and to be happy with him forever in heaven.

***Question:*** What is a sacrament?
***Answer:*** A sacrament is an outward sign instituted by God to give us grace.

Our understanding of sin was also clearly defined in black-and-white terms. Sins were counted and categorized as "mortal" and "venial." To commit a mortal sin was to "fall from God's grace" – and if one died without confessing that sin, one would go to Hell. (In fact, in those days, there were a lot of things that would send people to Hell!) The list of mortal sins – any one of which would take you out of the state of grace and assure you of eternal damnation – was depressingly long, and they were very easy to commit. Eating meat on a Friday, missing Mass on a Sunday, or holding back a mortal sin in Confession were among the most feared possibilities in my life, as a child and even as a young adult. With adolescence, there came a whole new array of opportunities for damnation, most of them related to sexual thoughts and actions.

Perhaps not surprisingly, we went to Confession frequently in those days, because living outside the state of grace was just too dangerous: one could die at any moment, and then one was lost forever – as the good Sisters told us again and again. We were taught that sin was forgiven in Confession, but that the punishment due to sin remained. To take away that punishment, one could "earn indulgences" – by going to Mass, saying certain prayers, or performing good works. While never officially taught by the Church, this doctrine implied in practice that you were expected to make up for your sins and thereby *earn* your way into heaven.

As a result of such teachings and practices, I grew up with a very legalistic image of God. My God was a judgmental God – a policeman in the sky. My God was an accountant God, who kept track of everything I did and expected me to make it all balance out – or else. Mine was not a warm and caring God... and that image was only reinforced by the behavior of my parents, who were not warm and demonstrative people. My father, a product of his old-world European culture, was authoritarian and strict; my mother was passive and expressed little emotion. Yet they were good people and, in their way, I'm sure they loved me... but I don't recall the words "I love you" ever being spoken in our house. So I grew up without an expressed or "felt" sense of being loved.

One day, when I was about five years old, a car drove up to our Northern Indiana farmhouse and two men got out. I remember a lot of crying and yelling – then the two men took "my papa" away. He spent the remaining twenty-five years of his life in a state mental hospital, and Mom was left alone to raise seven kids on a broken-down farm with no electricity, no telephone, no indoor plumbing, and no means of transportation.

Mom was from Alabama, the daughter of a dirt-poor sharecropper. After the eighth grade, she had to drop out of school to help work in the cotton fields. Mom was not a very emotional or expressive person: as a child, I never heard her say "I love you." But sometimes she would say "Jimmy's a good boy" – and it didn't take me long to equate approval with love.

As a child and as a teenager, I became determined to do everything right to get that approval. I tried to become the ideal kid: I did what I was told and I obeyed all the rules. The Church said it was a mortal sin to miss Mass on Sunday – so, at age twelve, I would often hitch-hike five miles into town to go to Mass. The Church said we were not to eat meat on Friday – so I would eat no food at all on Friday, just to be sure that I didn't make a mistake and accidentally eat some meat! And to be sure that I confessed everything, I kept a list of my sins. (Can you imagine a teenage boy trying to keep count of the number of times he thought about sex? I don't think I could do that, even as an old man!)

When I was around twelve years old, I found a book in my father's old desk – it was his Bible. And I began reading it, because doing that somehow seemed to put me in touch with Dad. I was still reading from it on a regular basis years later, when I left home as a young man.

But reading the Bible was not comforting to me. I found the stories in the Old Testament to be frightening, because it seemed that God was always punishing those who didn't obey him, casting plagues on innocent people, or striking people dead. That stern image of God was dramatically portrayed in Cecil B. DeMille's cinematic classic, *The Ten Commandments*. As a high-school student, I sat in a darkened theater and watched in horror as the Angel of Death (depicted as a rolling green mist) seeped into each house and took the life of the innocent first-born child of every Egyptian family. And I thought to myself, "Yeah, that's pretty much what I would expect from a God who would send a child to Hell for missing Mass on Sunday!"

That was the God I knew as a child and as a young adult!

But little did I know that, one day, a softball game would change my life.

"That's her," my friend indicated to me. "The one running for second base – she's your blind date!" I had already stood this girl up twice before, when friends tried to connect us at parties, but I decided that a picnic such as this one was a safe environment in which to meet her. Heck, I could always disappear into the woods if things didn't go well!

I thought she was a little dizzy – after all, who could take a bleached blonde seriously? And she thought I was a little boring – after all, who could have fun with a guy who wore dress shoes and black socks to a picnic? I also thought we had a whirlwind romance – because we got engaged after only knowing each other a year and a half! That seemed pretty quick to me; as I told my friends, "It takes me longer than that to buy a car!" But my fiancée, Helen, knew better. She had told her roommates on the day after the picnic: "I met the guy I'm going to marry!"

Now that we were engaged, I knew that, sooner or later, I'd have to take her to meet my Mom. The trip back home had never seemed so long – driving on Highway 29 and winding through the farmlands of northern Indiana, even the most direct route didn't feel like the "short" way this time. I had never brought a girl home before, and I was nervous. I was also wrestling with how to tell Helen our dark "family secret" – that my father had spent twenty-five years in a mental institution.

"I need to show you something!" I suddenly blurted out, as I swerved the car onto Highway 25 and drove to the Logansport State Hospital campus. It was a hot summer day as I walked with my fiancée to the center of the grounds... and it was lunchtime; the patients were emerging from the buildings by the hundreds from every direction. Some were talking to themselves, others were clinging to dolls, and many were screaming in anguish. With a bewildered look, Helen finally asked, "What is this place?" "Look around you," I replied in a stern voice, pointing to a thousand patients – "this is my earliest memory; this is my greatest fear. If you have any sense, you'll get in the car and go back to Indianap-" I never finished that sentence; instead, I felt her arms around me and I heard her say again and again, "I love you – I love you – I love you." And for the first time, I *felt* loved – and I knew my life would never be the same.

But my fears did not go quickly or gently into the night. The vengeful and frightening God of my youth still haunted me. But slowly, I started to become aware of the inconsistency between my feelings about God, and the love I felt for my wife and our two boys. Helen kept challenging my perception of God: "Would you send Jimmy to Hell for missing Mass?" she would ask me every time the subject came up. "What about Mark? Would you send him to Hell for eating meat on a Friday?" "Of course not!" I barked in frustration. "I love them!" "So, if you wouldn't treat your sons that way, why do you think God would treat them that way? Is your love greater than God's love?"

Helen's logic made sense (and I would later realize that Jesus himself used a similar comparison in Matthew 7:9-11) – but I was a "fundamentalist Catholic" back then, and nobody's word counted except that of a priest! One day, I happened to listen to a talk by Fr. Richard Rohr (the now-famous author and retreat master), in which he said: "God loves us and doesn't keep track of our sins. And not only that, you don't have to *earn* salvation – he gives it to you for free!" I had never heard such a thing said by a Catholic, much less a priest... still, my first response was "This guy must be nuts!"

But I couldn't escape the thought. What if he was right? *What if it was really true?*

I had to know. I yanked open my Bible and ripped into scripture with a vengeance, looking for all the passages that spoke of salvation as a gift. And – praise the Lord! – there were many such passages. And they all seemed to be aimed directly at me:

Jim, *Salvation is not the result of your own efforts, but God's gift to you.* (Ephesians 2:8-9)

Jim, *What my father wants is this – that all those he has given to me be saved.* (John 6:40)

Jim, *I am writing that you may know that you have eternal life.* (1 John 5:13)

Jim, *God's free gift is eternal life.* (Romans 4:16 & 6:23)

Jim, *God wants everyone to be saved.* (1Timothy 2:3)

Jim, *We have faith and are saved.* (Hebrews 10:39)

But surely, I thought, there is nothing like this in the Old Testament, where my God of vengeance lurks, waiting to pounce on my every slip-up! Yet I continued to read:

Jim, *Proclaim everyday the good news that He has saved us.* (Psalm 96)

Jim, *He does not punish us as we deserve, or repay us according to our sins.* (Psalm 103)

Jim, *If I kept a record of sins, who could stand?* (Psalm 130)

Jim, *Do not be afraid – I will save you. I have called you by name, and you are mine. See, I have written your name on the palm of my hand!* (Isaiah 43 & 49)

I was kneeling at my bedside now, with my head in my hands, sobbing uncontrollably as I felt the chains of my slavery to guilt and fear fall from my shoulders. And Mom's favorite hymn played through my mind:

*"T'was grace that taught my heart to fear / And grace my fears relieved / How precious did that grace appear / The hour I first believed!"*

### *The Room Where I Grew Up*

***Ecclesiastes 12:1, 6-7***

*Remember your God in the days of your youth before the silver cord is snapped, or the golden bowl is broken, or the pitcher is shattered at the fountain, or the wheel broken at the cistern, and the dust returns to the earth as it was, and the spirit returns to God who gave it.*

"My name is Jim... and I'm a workaholic!"

I've never had the opportunity to use that introduction, because there are no meetings for those with my addiction. It's defined as "dedication" in the business world, and it's honored as "service" in the world of ministry. I missed exactly one-and-a-half days of work in twenty-two years of employment; no one ever cared about that statistic but me – but, for years, I wore it like a badge of honor. I was completely unaware that it expressed how closely my work was connected to my self-esteem, and to my personal identity.

There are other examples of this close connection, of course: one Monday morning, I went to the office and found the parking lot empty and the doors locked! I returned home to relate this puzzling experience to my wife. "Uh, dear... most people don't work on *Labor Day!*" she explained.

My obsession with work still leaves me unchallenged for the "Jerk of the Year" award at social gatherings of family and friends when such stories are told. Jim, our oldest son was born with a slight case of jaundice, which prevented us from taking him home from the hospital on that Friday when my wife Helen was released. We were young and first-time parents; understandably, she was crying and very upset. It did seem strange – even to me – to leave the hospital without our new baby. But we were assured that he would be fine by Monday, and we could pick him up then.

As I got ready for work on Monday morning, my wife reminded me: "Don't forget, we're going to bring the baby home today!" "Honey," I replied, "can't you and your sister do that? I have sales calls to make!" (There is always an audible gasp when I tell this part of the story!) To make matters worse, I didn't even see the problem – I didn't understand why Helen was crying! My response didn't help much: "Honey, I'll see him tonight. I've got to go to work; I'm the *provider* for this family."

Fast forward twenty-plus years: it's 1992, and there is excitement in the house! Jim is well into college, and our second son, Mark, is now getting ready to leave home for college too. There is talk of dorm rooms, subject majors, and career choices. Helen is excited about her new career in nursing. Everyone is having fun... except me. I am sad!

Helen has always known me better than I know myself, but for years, her attempts to help me find value in things other than what I could "do" were largely fruitless. "You're sad," she told me (as she began yet another unsolicited counseling session), "because you let others define you. 'You are what you do' – you're a husband, a father, an accountant – and you buy into society's definitions and labels. The question is: who are you when those things are gone?" I'd heard it all before, so I brushed it off with an attempt at humor: "You're right, dear; I *am* an accountant – and I have to go to work in the morning! Good night!"

Some time later, I stood in the middle of the street as Mark drove away. I watched the "Go Purdue" sticker on the back of his car get smaller and smaller – until finally, it was a near-imperceptible speck. As I went back into the house, the hallway to his bedroom suddenly seemed very long. I walked those lonely steps and wondered, "How could a time we waited for so long, hurt so much?" I could almost hear the silence of his empty room. The very walls seemed to whisper the questions now, and they would not be dismissed with a flippant "good night." *You're not a provider anymore .... so who are you now?*

I sat in that empty room where our boys had hatched plans and their ponderings of life were broken with laughter as secrets were shared. "We really should have changed that wallpaper sooner," I mused. "He was too old for airplanes and trains." As I listened to the walls in my son's room, I knew that the issues were larger this time. It was clear that Helen could live without me; she had always been more independent than I liked to believe. It seemed I had three choices: I could live in an illusion, and play the role of provider to an empty house. I could find someone who needed a good provider, and get my needs met in my traditional way. Or I could redefine myself. I understood why so few choose that last option; either of the other choices would have been much easier.

Only someone who has gone through a mid-life transition can fully appreciate how painful a change it can be. As an accountant, I "closed the books" over 18,000 times; my work had become very routine. But those years cannot simply be dismissed; one does not walk away from the workbench of one's life with a simple wave of the hand! And, in the words of author and poet Alice Walker, one so anchored does not easily begin to "move to music that has not yet been written."

"Are you crazy? I *have* to work!" was my loud protest at my wife's suggestion that I go to school full time and get the college degree I had so often talked about. "Who are you providing for, dear? The boys are both in college, and I have my own career now." "I want to give the boys something to fall back on," I insisted. "The safety net I never had." "Is that your need or theirs?" Her questions were unrelenting. "Why don't we ask *them?*" she suggested. "Hey, Jim," she yelled across the room, "Dad's not going to school so he can provide you with a financial safety net!" "Oh no, you don't," came the booming reply from my older son, who was home for spring break. "You're not going to use *me* as your excuse! Dad, who are you kidding? You work because you're afraid of being poor!" "Am I *that* transparent?" I mumbled. "Does 'Mr. Cellophane' mean anything to you, Dad?"

"Well, I just can't do that," I continued to protest. "If I go back to school now, I'll be 56 years old when I graduate!" "And how old will you be if you *don't* graduate?" He continued the conversation with the confidence of one who knew he was too old to be sent to his room: "Color outside the lines, Dad!" "Where did you hear that, in one of those courses I paid for? I don't even know what that means – 'color outside the lines'..." "It means 'do your own thing,'" my wife replied, continuing her translation in my ear. "And it means he supports you, dummy!"

"Nothing is more important than a good education," my son went on. "And just because you have a Cum Laude wife, and two sons on the Dean's List – hey, there's no pressure!" And then his younger brother – also home for break – chimed in: "You get to meet a lot of girls, Dad. And history should be easy for you; you'll *remember* most of that stuff!" (*Why don't they just call in the neighbors and let everyone take a shot?* I lamented to myself.) "I *cannot* go back to school," I continued to insist. "I'd be so out of place. Why, I've got sweatshirts older than those kids! It's not going to happen!"

And yet...

It was a bright sunny morning as I walked across the Indianapolis campus of Indiana University for the first time – as a 53-year-old freshman – and looked at the downtown office buildings outlined against the sky. Those buildings, which were once my stronghold, now became a daily reminder of how much my life had changed. I wasn't sure where God's hand was in this new life I had begun, but I knew things would never be the same.

Slowly and often painfully, I began to move to the "music not yet written," as labels, images, and definitions began to fall to the ground. I could almost hear them shatter as they fell: provider, accountant, organizer. And new notes began to sound: student, scholar, writer, classmate, philosopher, husband, father.

One day we finally took down the model airplanes which were suspended from the ceiling of my younger son's room. We finally stripped the wallpaper and re-painted those walls.

And finally, I could laugh again – sitting in the room where I grew up.

**Reflection:**

**1.** What labels have you had to shed in order to become something more? What labels do you still need to shed... to become something more?

**2.** In your life, who has helped you realize your potential? How did they do so?

**3.** What truths about God have your children, grand- children, or other children taught you?

**How Sweet the Sound** **Ephesians 2:8-10**

*For it is by God's grace that you have been saved through faith. It is not the result of your own efforts, but God's gift, so that no one can boast about it. God has made us what we are, and in our union with Christ Jesus he has created us for a life of good deeds, which he has already prepared for us to do.*
(Good News translation)

"I'm not going to listen to any more of your sins!" the old priest barked at me through the screen of the confessional. I was eleven years old and had been confessing my "sins" for more than twenty minutes, taking up all the time allotted for Confession before Sunday Mass. "But I'm not finished," I started to whimper. "If I don't tell you everything, I could go to Hell – I won't be in the state of grace!"

My list was that of a frightened little boy, and it must have seemed endless to the old priest: *I said this, I thought that. I found a nickel and kept it without trying to find its rightful owner. I was distracted during Mass; I have trouble following the Latin. I may have committed a mortal sin by missing Mass last Sunday. I could have walked to town – it's only three miles if I walk down the railroad tracks – but it was raining. Is it a sin if I don't walk three miles to church in the rain?*

As a young boy and throughout my teenage years, I always tried to go to Confession just before Mass began. That way, I could sometimes make it to Communion before feeling that I had sinned again. That, of course, would mean that I had fallen from grace and was unworthy to receive the Eucharist. Sometimes, even so, I went to Communion because I was embarrassed not to go, because my mother and my siblings all knew that I had just gone to Confession. And in my mind, that resulted in yet another sin, this time a serious one: receiving Communion unworthily!

In all of this, the religious doctrine of "grace" and its rituals, which were supposed to bring peace and joy, brought me only fear and shame. As a child and well into young adulthood, trying to remain in the "state of grace" was a nightmare for me. I suffered constant anxiety and deep feelings of guilt. I rarely felt that I was in the state of grace beyond Wednesday following a weekend sacrament!

In my experience of the pre-Vatican Catholic Church, we put grace into two categories: Actual Grace and Spiritual Grace. And we spoke in terms of "gaining" and "losing" grace, and of being "in" or "not in" the state of grace. Grace was, in effect, moving in and out of our soul. And Sacraments were understood to be "channels" of God's grace, not simply an assurance of its enduring presence.

But the teachings of the Second Vatican Council, as well as scripture itself, have convinced me that sacramental Confession does not bring God's forgiveness into being, any more than Baptism or a kind act brings his love into being! Sacraments proclaim and enable us to receive and celebrate a love that is already ours, as expressed in God's unending and ever-present grace. In the spirit of Vatican II, a Sacrament was commonly defined as "an outward sign of an inward reality." In other words, we come to Confession (now called "Reconciliation") already forgiven! And the change of name reflects this new understanding: we do not come to confess our sins so that God will forgive us – we come to reconcile ourselves to a God who has *already* forgiven us!

Simply put, we don't go to Reconciliation to "get" or "obtain" forgiveness; we go to Reconciliation to verbalize our sins, which forces us to acknowledge them and makes them more real to us. We go to Reconciliation to hear God's forgiveness announced by the confessor, who by his presence, assures us of God's love and mercy, and reconciles us to the community. We receive the Sacrament of Reconciliation to *celebrate* God's forgiveness – which is already ours. God does not wait for us to confess, and we are *never* in a state of not being forgiven!

In the story of the Prodigal Son in St. Luke's gospel (Luke 15: 11-32), the father shows no interest in his son's confession of sin. He accepts the son back immediately, no questions asked; the young man is not even through his brief rehearsed speech before the family ring is back on his finger and a robe is on his shoulders. In Jesus' own dealings with sinners and his teachings about forgiveness, "compensation" or "satisfaction" is never mentioned, much less made a requirement for being received back into God's love or experiencing the gift of his grace.

After many years that are still very painful to recall (and much subsequent counseling), I have come to believe that grace speaks to our *relationship* with God. From God's side of the equation, we cannot even think in limiting terms like "more" or "less" – it is just total, ever-present, amazing grace. If there are any limits to grace, they lie on *our* side of the equation! It is only there that we can properly speak in terms of more or less – in describing our willingness to *accept* God's gift of grace.

Thanks be to God that his grace is always present, and that he does not give it only to take it away again – not even for a moment! It is always there. All we have to do is accept it.

When I recall that, I can still hear Mom humming that Baptist hymn as she worked around the old farmhouse: *"Amazing grace / How sweet the sound / That saved and set me free!"*

**Reflection:**

**1.** What was your experience of Reconciliation (going to Confession) as a child? Has your experience of this sacrament changed as an adult? If so, in what way?

**2.** How do you understand "grace" in your life today?

**3.** What experience has taught you the meaning of forgiveness?

### *Born Again* *John 3:1-4*

*Now there was a man of the Pharisees named Nicodemus, a ruler of the Jews. This man came to Jesus by night and said to him, "Rabbi, we know that you are a teacher come from God, for no one can do these signs that you do unless God is with him." Jesus answered him, "Truly, truly, I say to you, unless one is born again he cannot see the kingdom of God." Nicodemus said to him, "How can a man be born when he is old? Can he enter a second time into his mother's womb and be born?"*

There is a classic tale in the Buddhist tradition that seems to speak to this gospel passage. "A man is walking along a high road and sees a great river: its near bank is dangerous and frightening, but its far bank is calm and safe. So he builds a raft and paddles to the other shore. Now suppose he puts the raft on his head and carries it wherever he walks. What would you say? Would he be using the raft in an appropriate way? No; a reasonable person would understand that the raft has been useful to him in crossing the river and arriving safely on the other side – but, once he has arrived, it is best to leave the raft behind and walk on without it."

In the same way, the story implies, all truths should be used to cross over to a new vision or to reach a deeper understanding. But, like a raft that has been useful, some old beliefs should not be held on to once you have reached the other side!

Nicodemus is a good man, and a would-be disciple of Jesus; he is a seeker of truth. Nicodemus is also a "leader of the Jews," and "a teacher of Israel" (John 3:1). But Nicodemus continues to "carry his raft," so he has a hard time understanding Jesus. He continues to cling to those beliefs that have served him in the past: his need for absolutes, the security he finds in simple answers, his obsession with the letter of the law, and his attitude that things *must* be a certain way. Nicodemus still carries on the rituals and is weighed down by the law.

Jesus was trying to get Nicodemus to "cross over" to the next level of faith. But, when Jesus spoke of rebirth – that one must be born again to enter the kingdom of God – Nicodemus could only understand it one way... literally. A physical rebirth? "No," Jesus responds, "someone who is reborn spiritually knows the experience as surely as one who has been refreshed by an invisible breeze. How can a respected rabbi among the Jews not know this?" (John 3:10)

Nicodemus does not "know this" because his beliefs have blinded him to other possibilities. And sometimes our beliefs blind us, too. We often think God can only work in the ways that *we* expect him to work – that God is only present through *our* rituals, that he can only forgive sins confessed to *our* ministers, or that he can only save those who believe *our* way!

We are still carrying our raft!

Jesus seems to be saying to Nicodemus: your beliefs have gotten you this far, but it's time to cross over and realize that you can't contain God! You can't limit God to *your* rules, *your* laws, *your* rituals, *your* customs, or *your* way of thinking. God is bigger than all of that. God is bigger than any box you can draw, greater than any limit you can imagine. You don't need that raft anymore – so lay it down! Let go of everything you "know," and experience God in a new way. *Be born again!*

Being born again – that is, the promise of new life – is not simply an add-on to our old life. As Jesus says elsewhere in scripture, you can't put new wine into old wineskins. New life always involves movement, change, risk, and loss. New life means that something has to die. And it may mean letting go of some cherished beliefs that have, in the past, served us well.

During uncertain times, there is a particularly strong tendency to cling to that which we "know," to hang on to the simple answers that give us our illusions of security and control. In uncertain times, it may seem even more difficult to lay down our "raft." But that is often what we must do in order to continue our journey.

What raft are you carrying today? Are you willing to let go of everything you "know" so you may have new life – and be born again?

**Reflection:**

**1.** What beliefs are you holding on to that hinder your growth? What can you do to change those beliefs?

**2.** What belief or conviction have you let go of in the past, and in what way did it affect your relationships and/or your spiritual growth?

**3.** In what way(s) do you sometimes "limit" God in your life? What can you do to begin to go beyond those limits?

**Barefoot in the Sand** **Luke 6:37-38**

*Judge not, and you will not be judged; condemn not, and you will not be condemned; forgive, and you will be forgiven; give, and it will be given to you. Good measure, pressed down, shaken together, running over, will be put into your lap. For with the measure you use it will be measured back to you.*

"What are those silly-looking things?" I asked my wife, as we walked on the beach in one of our favorite vacation spots. "They're water shoes," she explained. "People wear them so they don't hurt their feet on stones or shells, and the holes in the shoes let the water run out." "I guess I didn't get the e-mail," I mumbled (a phrase I use when it seems that everyone except me is aware of some new fashion or trend).

As we continued our walk, I overheard the protest of a little boy whose mother was trying to get *him* to wear water shoes! "But Mom," he protested, "if I don't go barefoot, how can I leave footprints in the sand?"

The above scripture passage seemingly presents a barrage of promises in the structure of a barter or exchange: "Stop condemning, and you won't be condemned. Forgive, and you will be forgiven. Give, and it will be given to you." It sounds like the classic *quid pro quo*: if you do this, you'll get that. And it seems to imply that God's gifts are things we must earn, or things that are distributed sparingly by a tit-for-tat Father... unless, of course, we look more deeply into this passage's meaning.

Our God is so much bigger than that! His grace is not given to us only under certain conditions, and then withheld from us at other times; no, his gifts are *always* "pressed down, shaken together, and overflowing"! (Luke 6:38) And God's gifts are *always* ours to have – they are limited only by our openness to receive them.

They are ours if we are open enough to accept others without judgment.

They are ours if we are open enough to let go of our anger and forgive those who have wronged us.

They are ours if we are open enough to allow ourselves to be vulnerable.

They are ours – if we are open enough to take off our shoes and walk barefoot in the sand!

How about you? Can you give up control of what you have created and run freely in God's grace? Are you willing to risk vulnerability and rejection as you offer forgiveness to those who have hurt you? Are you willing to share your troubles so that others may see your heart?

Are you willing to go barefoot... so you can leave footprints in the sand?

**Reflection:**

**1.** What in your life do you need to give control of to God, so you can experience God's grace?

**2.** To whom do you need to offer forgiveness in your life?

**3.** How does sharing your troubles allow others to see your heart?

### *Moving the Fence* *Matthew 23:16-19*

*Woe to you, blind guides, who say, "If one swears by the temple, it means nothing, but if one swears by the gold of the temple, one is obligated." Blind fools, which is greater, the gold, or the temple that made the gold sacred? And you say, "If one swears by the altar, it means nothing, but if one swears by the gift on the altar, one is obligated." You blind ones, which is greater, the gift, or the altar that makes the gift sacred?*

**O**ne of the most beautiful images in scripture is Jacob's dream of the ladder (or stairway) to heaven: God opened a door for Jacob that brought him and his people into a new relationship. In the above scripture story, Jesus stuns the local religious leaders by asserting that they have *closed* that door – not only for themselves, but for others as well!

The word "woe" is also translated as "alas"; it is as much an expression of sorrowful pity as it is of anger. Jesus was angry and disappointed with the religious leaders because they had failed to listen to God's word and had misled the people they were supposed to guide. "Blind guides," he says, you don't even understand what's important – you yourselves miss the point, so how can you lead others? Jesus then gives a series of examples to show the many ways in which they were misguided. In their zeal to win converts, they imposed unnecessary and burdensome rules which obscured the more important aspects of religion, such as love of God and love of neighbor. They were leading people to legalism, rather than to God.

How often we, too, close the door to God, both for ourselves and for others, by insisting on "the rules" – as if God, who created the universe, can't operate outside the box *we* have drawn! Legalism looks for ways to exclude people, ways to close the door. God finds ways to include us; he keeps the door open.

In pre-Vatican II days, there were restrictions about who could be buried in a Catholic cemetery: public sinners, those married outside the church, etc., were excluded. Most church-owned cemeteries had some type of fence around them, so reference was made to those who were "buried outside the fence."

There was a story about a Pastor who was deeply troubled by these restrictions, which required someone he knew to be buried "outside the fence." Finally, he could stand it no longer: in the middle of the night, he got up, went to the cemetery, and moved the fence so it included the person who was excluded by "the law."

That's what God does: by his grace... he moves the fence for us!

**Reflection:**

**1.** What groups in our church or society are "outside the fence" today? What civil or church law do you think should be changed to include those "outside the fence"? What effect would that change have?

**2.** Give an example in your life when you disregarded a rule, law, teaching or societal norm to include someone who was being excluded.

**3.** What in your life do you need to change to "open the door" for others?

**Grace to You** **2 Thessalonians 1:1-3**

*Paul, Silvanus, and Timothy, To the church of the Thessalonians in God our Father and the Lord Jesus Christ: Grace to you and peace from God our Father and the Lord Jesus Christ. We ought always to give thanks to God for you, brothers, as is right, because your faith is growing abundantly, and the love of every one of you for one another is increasing.*

With apologies to Johnny Carson, the answer is: Fulton Sheen and Richard Rohr!

Now, the envelope please... "Name the two authors who had the most influence on Jim Welter's spiritual life."

*Falling Upward* is a fairly recent book by Richard Rohr that appeals to me on several levels: first, as far as Rohr's works go, it's a pretty easy read. And secondly, it hits me where I live – that is, in the "second half" of my spiritual life. Rohr helps us see how differently we often look at life from its "second half"; for many of us, the second half of our life gives us a different view of what is important. Much of this change in focus simply comes from our situation: in the second half of life, we are no longer focusing on getting kids through school, building careers, establishing our identity, and all of those other "first half" concerns. And so we have time to consider more deeply many things we used to take for granted – such as Paul's first line of greeting in 2 Thessalonians: "Grace to you."

For much of my life, I described myself as a self-made man. I crawled across onion fields when I was in the first grade to earn seven cents an hour; in high school, I walked five miles into town to earn thirty cents an hour working at the local store. As a young man, I lived in a cold-water flat in Chicago and walked to work to avoid bus fare – all to save money so I could go to business school. So, for many years afterwards, I held a lot of anger toward those who seemed to have had life handed to them, those born with the proverbial silver spoon in their mouth. They had no idea what I had gone through to get that nameplate on my desk!

*Grace to you!*

From my "second half" viewpoint, I see things very differently. Now I realize that much of what I was able to accomplish was made possible, not by my efforts, but through the gifts of others: a good mother who instilled a work ethic in me, a sister who believed in me, teachers who encouraged me, a God who gave me intelligence and good health, etc. I now understand that no one truly does it alone; we all receive help from others.

*Grace to you!*

The recognition that no one does it alone has carried over into the "second half" of my spiritual life as well: I no longer think of Heaven as a prize to be won, or something I have to work for, gain, or earn in some way. Rather, I believe salvation is what St. Paul says it is throughout his writings: God's free gift. The idea that we are saved by grace which frees us to do good works stands in sharp contrast to my "first half" spirituality! Yes, I still do many of the same things, such as read the Bible and go to church – but I now have a different motive. I no longer work in God's vineyard because I "have to"; I work in his vineyard because I "get to"!

*Grace to you!*

Grace is the central theme in most of Paul's letters; Ephesians 2:8, Romans 6:23, and Hebrews 10:39 are but a few examples.

Grace as the means to our salvation is also a core theological belief of most Christians. Yet nowhere in the New Testament does Jesus use the word "grace"! And I think the reason for that has to do with the nature of grace. It's like trying to explain a joke: suddenly the story is no longer funny, and it ceases to *be* a joke. Similarly, when one tries to define music or explain dance, something gets lost in the translation. And when we try to define grace, it ceases to be grace and becomes something else: dogma, or doctrine, or religion.

Grace can be experienced or observed – but, in a sense, it cannot be defined and still be grace. So Jesus doesn't talk about it or try to define it; rather, he *demonstrates* grace. We see grace at work in the story of the prodigal son, in the parable of the tenants in the vineyard, in the incident of the woman being stoned for adultery, and in the encounter with the woman at the well. Although perhaps Jesus' words do hint at grace indirectly when he says, "The wind blows where it wishes, and you hear its sound, but you do not know where it comes from or where it goes. So it is with everyone who is born of the Spirit." (John 3:8)

Grace is a difficult concept for us to grasp because it is such a great gift! It leaves nothing for us to "do" to affect our salvation; we need only accept the gift which will lead us to do good works. Paul explains this in his instructions to the Ephesians (2:9): "He has created us for a life of good deeds which he has already prepared for us to do." Paul seems to believe that the greatest danger to our salvation is that we won't trust in God's plan! He cautions the Philippians to "Work out your salvation in fear and trembling" (Philippians 2:12) – but, by this, he doesn't mean that we should fear the God of grace, but that we should fear we won't *trust* in his grace. What we should fear is giving in to the temptation to come up with our *own* plan, by trying to "do" something that will contribute to our salvation or give us some added assurance beyond God's word.

In my "second half" spirituality, I believe with St. Paul that grace is God's greatest gift. So my prayer for you is that of Paul: "Grace to you from God our Father and the Lord Jesus Christ!"

**Reflection:**

**1.** Has your understanding of grace changed as you've gotten older? If so, in what way has it changed?

**2.** How does your current understanding of grace affect your life?

**3.** How do you demonstrate grace in your life?

**_I'm Still Here_** **_Acts 16:25-28_**

*About midnight Paul and Silas were praying and singing hymns to God, and the prisoners were listening to them, and suddenly there was a great earthquake, so that the foundations of the prison were shaken. And immediately all the doors were opened, and everyone's bonds were unfastened. When the jailer woke and saw that the prison doors were open, he drew his sword and was about to kill himself, supposing that the prisoners had escaped. But Paul cried with a loud voice, "Do not harm yourself, for we are still here."*

"I'm still here," a mother whispers to her sick child. "I'm still here," a husband whispers to his dying spouse. "I'm still here," an employee greets a co-worker. "I'm still HERE!" says the frustrated spouse who is unable to verbally express his or her feelings. In whatever way they are said, those words speak of faithfulness, commitment, and love.

Its August 10, 1945, and I'm five years old. My older siblings are six, seven, eight, nine, and ten. My baby brother is just six months old. Suddenly, a car pulls into the driveway. Our farm is on a dirt road, five miles from town, and over a mile from the nearest neighbor; we don't see many cars out here. Two men get out of the car, and I remember a lot of yelling and crying. And they take my father away. He will spend the remaining 25 years of his life in a state mental institution.

I can't begin to imagine how my mother must have felt as she faced the daunting task of raising seven kids alone, without the benefits of running water, electricity, a telephone, or any means of transportation. But she chose to say, "I'm still here!"

Mom wrote the book on commitment. She wrote it with countless items of clothing scrubbed one at a time in a ten-gallon tub. She wrote it in wood split, coal hauled, gardens hoed, meals cooked, tears shed, and hurts kissed away. Mom was never bitter about her difficult circumstances. She would often say, "I'm here, so this must be what God wants me to do."

Paul and Silas did not choose to be in prison; circumstances placed them there. There is an earthquake, their chains are broken, and they have a chance to escape. In that time and culture, if a prisoner escaped, the punishment to the jailer was death – so Paul and Silas choose to stay because of the harm that would come to their captor if they left. Paul shouted with a loud voice, "We are still here!" And the jailer, about to literally fall on his sword, hears those saving words and rejoices. Those words give him hope and bring him new life.

For most of us, being a Christian isn't dramatic; it's often just living the life and saying, "I'm still here." Perhaps there is an area of your life from which you would like to escape, but in which you have instead chosen to stay and say, "I'm still here." Maybe it's a troubled marriage, or a difficult relationship; maybe you're dealing with sickness, grief, or loss, or perhaps it's just the grind of daily living.

"I'm still here!" Those words convey love, and give strength; they are powered by grace and open us to new life.

"I'm still here!"

To whom will you say those words today?

**Reflection:**

**1.** In our society, why is it sometimes so hard to make a commitment to something or someone?

**2.** In what ways have you said "I'm still here" in your life?

**3.** How can we teach commitment to our children, grandchildren, and all the children who will be the adults of tomorrow?

***You Don't Know Me*** ***Hosea 11:3-4***

*Yet it was I who taught Ephraim to walk, who took them in my arms; I drew them with human cords, with bands of love; I fostered them like one who raises an infant to his cheeks; Yet, though I stooped to feed my child, they did not know that I was their healer.*

The green Baltimore Catechism books of the pre-Vatican Catholic world were written in question-and-answer form, and our Catechism classes in the 1950s consisted almost entirely of an effort to memorize the answers in that book. It was a pretty black-and-white approach: there was no doubt, discussion, hedging, or uncertainty in the answers that the catechism provided. These were *the answers* – period. The book's picture of Jesus with his arms around a sinner, above the caption "Jesus loves you WHEN you are sorry for your sins," didn't help much either; it was pretty easy to develop an image of a stern and legalistic God.

In Catechism class, I was Sister Gabriel's prize student. I always knew the answers, and I came from that experience knowing all about God. Yes, I knew all *about* God... yet I did not *know* God. I was well into adulthood before I could even bring myself to pray to God as "Father." Surely, I am one for whom Hosea writes: "Yet, though I stooped to feed my child, he did not know me" (Hosea 11:3-4).

It is summer, 1967. The visiting room of the state hospital in Logansport, Indiana, is stark. Sound echoes from the plain tile floor and voices return from the bare walls. My father has been in this place for twenty-five years now. We are visiting today. The quiet is broken, as a woman enters the room pushing a wheelchair. In it, she transports the deformed and helpless body of her son. Her eyes meet mine. Her pain outweighs my own; her son is my age. I turn away. They sit near us. This young man has a twin brother who is perfectly normal. There is another brother, too, and a sister. But they have not seen this plain floor, these bare walls; they do not come to visit. But this mother has driven sixty-five miles today. She has driven sixty-five miles every Saturday, for sixteen years, to be with her son.

Her cross is especially heavy today: her son is restless, and she struggles to feed him. Suddenly, he knocks the tray from her hands. Mashed potatoes and gravy cover his clothes. Meatloaf slides to the floor; the green beans add a strange color. Only a mother knows. She begins to clean him up, as she must have done a thousand times before. Quietly, she sobs. And I hear her whisper to her son: "I gave you life. I have fed you all these years. I love you. And you don't even know me!"

I wonder how often God, our loving Father, could say that of us: "I gave you life... I have fed you all these years... I love you... and you don't even know me."

How will you seek to know your Father today?

**Reflection:**

**1.** What experience, person or event in your life has helped you to "know" Jesus?

**2.** Why is it important that you continue the journey and know Jesus more fully?

**3.** How do you help others to know Jesus?

***Weeds and Wheat*** ***Matthew 13:27-29***

*The slaves of the householder came to him and said, "Master, did you not sow good seed in your field? Where have the weeds come from?" He answered, "An enemy has done this." His slaves said to him, "Do you want us to go and pull them up?" He replied, "No, if you pull up the weeds you might uproot the wheat along with them."*

When I was growing up on the farm, our garden was a major source of food for our family. We were a family of seven being raised by a single mother, and money was very tight; the garden was the best way to stretch a dollar. We grew a lot of beans, and we pulled a lot of weeds. As children, it wasn't always clear to us what was a plant and what was a weed, and we would get in trouble if we pulled up the plants. So, when in doubt, I would call my older sister Fran over and ask her, "Is this a plant or a weed?" Fran always knew. Sometimes she would say it was a weed, but that I should leave it alone: "It's too close to the plant; if you pull the weed, you'll kill the plant."

This parable from Matthew is about judgment. It cautions us not to judge before the play is done, before the fat lady sings, before the harvest comes. In the meantime, "the rain falls on the just and the unjust alike." The weeds and the wheat grow side by side; they are all part of the field, and to root out the weeds at this stage would destroy the wheat along with them. We must have patience. We must wait for the harvest.

On another level, I think we are also being called to an acceptance of our own humanness. In every heart, there are weeds and wheat, good and evil, light and shadow. *Make Friends With Your Shadow* was a popular spiritual book a decade or two ago. In it, the author suggested that we shouldn't strive to root out or deny our shadow side, but instead make friends with it. That is, recognize it, name it, and accept it as part of us, part of the field of our being. All the various twelve-step programs also recognize this need.

I've always been a control freak; it's my "original sin"! But it's such a basic trait in me that if, by some miracle, I could root that out of my personality, I would no longer be *me* – and all that is good and worthwhile about being me would also perish. Pulling the weed would destroy the wheat! So I must learn to accept the weeds in me – but, it is said, "If you can name it, you can tame it!" So, by recognizing my faults, flaws, and shortcomings, I can – with God's help – tame and harness them. I may even be able to turn them to a good purpose (control freaks make great administrators, business managers, and accountants!) Maybe that's why God allows such burdens to remain in our lives – so that, as we strive to overcome them, we become stronger, more loving people. An ancient Tibetan prayer even *asks* that we be granted "appropriate difficulties and sufferings"... so our hearts may be freed from selfishness and awakened to compassion for others.

This is our challenge and our struggle; our goal and our goodness; our cross and our crown.

Fran has been gone for more than fifteen years now. I miss her today. As I look at my life, I want to call her over one more time and ask, "Is this a plant... or a weed?"

**Reflection:**

**1.** What "weed" in your life has also proven to be a benefit to you?

**2.** How have you learned to tame that "weed"?

**3.** How has something that you have struggled with in yourself helped you become more compassionate toward others?

***What Must I Do?*** ***Matthew 19:16-22***

*And behold, a man came up to him, saying, "Teacher, what good deed must I do to have eternal life?" And he said to him, "Why do you ask me about what is good? There is only one who is good. If you would enter life, keep the commandments." He said to him, "Which ones?" And Jesus said, "You shall not murder, You shall not commit adultery, You shall not steal, You shall not bear false witness, Honor your father and mother, and, You shall love your neighbor as yourself." The young man said to him, "All these I have kept. What do I still lack?" Jesus said to him, "If you would be perfect, go, sell what you possess and give to the poor, and you will have treasure in heaven; and come, follow me." When the young man heard this he went away sad, for he had many possessions.*

**W**e tend to remember "firsts" in our lives... and the first person I ever fired was a young man named Dave. Dave was a "man about town," a "party animal"; Dave never saw a skirt he didn't chase. (My problem with Dave was that he didn't distinguish between work-time and play-time.) One day, on a coffee break, the group was talking about the Bible. And out of the blue, Dave casually said, "I don't read the Bible." Among the snickers and chuckles at such an obvious statement, I said, "Ok, Dave, I'll bite: why don't you read the Bible?" "Because if I did," Dave replied, "I'd have to change the way I live!" The group went silent. We were stunned by his honesty and convicted by his statement.

How often do we read scripture, but exclude ourselves from the story? We exclude ourselves because if we didn't – we would have to change the way *we* live! And this gospel passage is a classic example: it's so easy – and tempting – to dismiss the passage by saying: "I'm not rich; it doesn't apply to me!" Or "I don't really want to be 'perfect,' so I don't have to sell all that I have." And of course, we're quick to point out that Jesus had rich friends – and they didn't sell all *they* had!

The uncomfortable truth is that Jesus doesn't leave much "wiggle room" when it comes to how we deal with wealth. The admonition to "sell all you have" is found in all three synoptic gospels! And, to complicate matters even more, the apostles seem to take the statement literally, even questioning the adequacy of their own leaving everything. "See, we have left everything and followed you. What will we have?" (Matthew 19:27) And elsewhere, Timothy goes so far as to say that wealth can lead us "to ruin and destruction" and that we should "flee from it"! (1 Timothy 6:9-11)

Throughout the gospels, Jesus is very cautious about wealth and continually issues warnings against its dangers and temptations: "You can't serve both God and Mammon (the ancient personification of riches)!" To Jesus, it's about choices. And the real issue isn't wealth itself; it's about what we become as we seek and amass wealth, and the lengths to which we go, and tactics we use, to gain and protect it. The issue is how much we come to depend on it, the extent to which it separates us from those in need, and how it ends up dominating our lives. An ancient Eastern proverb expresses the danger well: "Wealth enters the house as a slave (we use it to serve our basic needs)... then it becomes a guest (we become comfortable with it and begin to cater to it)... then it becomes the Master (it controls our life and we do everything for it)."

The Greek word *teleios* (which is usually translated as "perfect") doesn't mean being without sin; rather, it means giving undivided devotion to God. The young man's problem wasn't so much his wealth as it was his divided loyalties! And Jesus is calling him to a decision. The very title by which the man is identified underscores the issue: "a rich young man." His possessions identify him! His wealth defines him! And Jesus asks him to change his identity. Jesus asks and invites him to become something *more* than simply "a rich young man." But in the end, the young man "went away sad, for he had many possessions" (Matthew 19:22).

How about you? Will you let this gospel passage change your life? Will you put aside your desire for wealth and possessions, and the divided loyalties it causes? Will you accept Jesus' request to change your identity, and accept his invitation to become something more than you are?

Or will you walk away sad?

**Reflection:**

**1.** What do you feel identifies you?

**2.** What do you feel divides your loyalties from God?

**3.** What "possessions" (i.e., material goods, beliefs, attitudes, obsessions) do you need to "sell" so you may walk more closely with the Lord?

***New Wineskins*** ***Mark 2:21-22***

*No one sews a piece of unshrunk cloth on an old garment. If he does, the patch tears away from it, the new from the old, and a worse tear is made. And no one puts new wine into old wineskins. If he does, the wine will burst the skins—and the wine is destroyed, and so are the skins. But new wine is for fresh wineskins.*

"What do you think would happen if you started shaving on the left side of your face in the morning, instead of the right?"

My counselor asked me that question at the end of an especially stressful session. And she didn't let up: "And what catastrophe do you think might take place if you took a different route to work? And if your shoes aren't lined up beside your bed at night, do you think they will still be there in the morning?" She was trying to get me to examine the "why" of my behavior, so the life changes I said I wanted could take place.

Knowing how difficult dealing with even small changes are for so many people, perhaps we can begin to understand the kind of disruption that occurs in many lives when new knowledge erupts, new people arrive, new songs are sung, new leaders emerge, illness disrupts, death looms, or there is suddenly an empty place at the table. Our resistance to change starts deep within, as a basic fear: fear of pain, fear of failure, or the fear of not being in control of events.

Paradoxically, we also build our lives on change: we raise children, go to school, learn new skills, take new jobs, get married, move into new houses, vote in elections, and dream of a better world. Yet the actual occurrence of change often leaves us fearful, defensive, and fighting to preserve the status quo – to preserve what we know, and the place where we are comfortable.

This resistance to change is what Jesus is dealing with when he speaks of "new wineskins" in the above scripture passage. Jesus warns his disciples about the problem of the status quo, or a closed mind that refuses to learn new things. To make his point, Jesus uses an image familiar to his audience: new and old wineskins. In the time of Jesus, wine was stored in wineskins, not bottles. New wine poured into a skin was still fermenting, and the gases created by that process exerted pressure on the skin. New wineskins were elastic enough to take the pressure, but old wineskins burst easily because they were hard and rigid.

What did Jesus mean by this comparison? Are we to reject the old in place of the new?

Yes and no. Jesus uses the wedding feast to make his point: just as there is a proper place and a right time for fasting and for feasting, so there is a proper place for the old as well as for the new. We shouldn't cling to the old just because it's comfortable, just because "we've always done it that way," nor should we embrace the new just because it's a novelty. Both old and new have their value – but sometimes the two don't mix. Most often, we just can't have it both ways: to experience the new, we have to let go of the old.

We simply can't be in two places at once! With physical changes, no one questions such a simple principle. But in emotional or psychological change, it's not as obvious or as easy – but it's still true: you can't cling to your fears *and* trust in God. You can't harbor resentment *and* be forgiven. You can't be selfish *and* love freely. You can't seek to control everything *and* be open to the Spirit. You can't serve God *and* money. You must let go of one in order to embrace the other. *"You can't pour new wine into an old wineskin."*

Scripture seems to be saying that God doesn't want us to hold rigidly to the past; God wants our minds and hearts to be like new wineskins, ready to receive the new wine of self-knowledge, vulnerability, and deeper relationships. God wants us to be open and ready to receive the Holy Spirit, which means always being open to something new that will make us stretch and grow, so we can become who we are truly meant to be.

How will you open your mind and heart to God today?

**Reflection:**

**1.** What image of God did you have to let go of in order to deepen your spiritual life?

**2.** Is change hard for you? Why or why not? Is change easy for you? Why or why not?

**3.** What growth have you experienced in your spiritual life that required a change in an attitude or belief?

### *God Is One* **Romans 3:28-30**

*For we hold that one is justified by faith apart from works of the law. Or is God the God of Jews only? Is he not the God of Gentiles also? Yes, of Gentiles also, since God is one—who will justify the circumcised by faith and the uncircumcised through faith.*

**M**y wife loves to travel (as do I, albeit with a little less passion). One of her favorite sayings is: "I am not the same person having seen the moon shine on the other side of the world." And wherever we go, Helen likes to "get authentic," meet the locals, and see how they live. In my best Zen voice, I tell her: "Honey, I will go with you as long as the waters flow – and the toilets flush!"

Our concept of God is certainly challenged as we travel and meet people in different lands. It makes St. Paul's words in the above passage come alive, for he reminds us that *no one* – not any single individual, culture, or faith – has an exclusive claim on God... "for God is one."

"This mountain is holy," our Chinese guide said to me as we stood on Temple Mountain outside of Beijing, China, one day. "We come here to pray," he continued. "What?" I replied in amazement. "I thought your people were atheistic Communists – so who are you praying to?" He extended both arms and, turning in a half circle, gestured at the beautiful mountains, the trees, the rocks, the clouds, and the sun, and said, "We are praying to whoever made all this!" (The "unknown God" that St. Paul talks about [Acts 17:23], I thought to myself.)

*God is one!*

An unplanned 4th of July getaway found us looking for somewhere go to Mass in Danville, KY, a few years ago. We were delighted to find St. Peter and Paul Parish: the people were friendly, the liturgy was wonderful, the music was lively, the homily was humorous and powerful – and the popular young pastor was Korean! "We have had a request for a special closing song for the holiday," he announced at the end of Mass. "We will sing 'God Bless America.' But you can only sing it if you sing one of my favorites also – 'God Bless Korea'!"

*God is one!*

Cairo, Egypt, 2010. Our Islamic friends Rougy and Ossama have shown us what thirty-somethings like to do on a lazy Saturday in Cairo – including drinking pigeon soup for lunch. "Would you like to go to Temple?" Ossama asked me as the call to prayer echoed through the marketplace. "God is one – we call him 'Allah,'" he said quietly.

"God is one – we call him 'Father,'" I replied. "Which way to the Temple?"

**Reflection:**

**1.** How has your idea of God been stretched by some person, place, or expression?

**2.** What does the statement "God is one" mean to you? How does it inform your Christian life?

**3.** What does "being saved" mean to you? If "God is one," how do you think he reaches out to those of other nations, cultures, or faiths?

## *The Second Chapter:*

# How Sweet the Sound

### *The Rivers of Babylon* *Psalm 137:1-4*

*By the rivers of Babylon, there we sat down; there we wept, when we remembered Zion. On the willows there we hung up our harps. For there our captors required of us songs, and our tormentors, mirth, saying, "Sing us a song of Zion!" How can we sing a song to the Lord in a foreign land?*

**I'**m delighted that my dear friend, the Reverend Doctor Audrey Borschel, agreed to write the foreword to this book. Audrey was one of the first people I met when I came to St. Monica Parish as Pastoral Associate and Business Manager in 1995. My mother had died earlier that year, and a few weeks after, my sister Fran had also died. I happened to walk through the Narthex of the church one day as Audrey was going into the Pastor's office. Our eyes met for only an instant, but in that moment, I knew that she too was grieving.

Some weeks later, when the Pastor formally introduced us, I learned that Audrey's son, Nick, had died that year. We (along with some other parishioners) founded the St. Monica Bereavement Ministry, and a friendship began. As the years passed and our friendship grew, the parallels in our lives continued – to an extent that almost seemed uncanny. Audrey became a Pastoral Associate in a neighboring parish and, after a few years and considerable struggle, she resigned from that ministry. Within a few months and under some painful circumstances, I, too resigned from my pastoral position at St. Monica. And the similarities didn't stop: I wrote a book, and Audrey later wrote a book. Audrey was diagnosed with cancer and, a few years later, I was diagnosed with cancer, as well. "If Audrey ever hit the lottery," I once remarked to my wife, "*we'd* probably get rich!"

During some of those difficult times, Audrey and I would meet for lunch to support each other and pray together. Sometimes we would just sit in silence on the deck of our favorite lunch spot on the banks of the White River, oblivious to the people around us. We could feel the warmth of the sun and hear the wind in the trees as the waters of the White River gently flowed by. In those moments, the real world seemed far away.

"There's the River of Babylon," Audrey quietly said one day. Our eyes met and our hands touched. I knew the passage by heart: "By the rivers of Babylon, we sat down; there we wept, when we remembered Zion... How can we sing to the Lord in a foreign land?"

How indeed, I wondered, can we sing in this foreign land of sadness and uncertainty? How can we sing in this place that is not of our choosing? How can we sing in this abyss of dashed hopes and broken dreams?

"You can't preach as you walk, if you don't walk as you preach." Audrey's often-repeated quote reminds me that it's from my unemployment that I can speak to the jobless. It's from my cancer that I can touch the heart of those who know illness and fear. It's from being without food that I can understand the plight of the hungry and the homeless. And it's from years of being weighed down by guilt that I can speak of belief and grace.

My friend continues to inspire me. Even now she walks the road of life-threatening cancer preaching about God's love and singing of his amazing grace.

God loves you, Audrey – and so do I.

**Reflection:**

**1.** From what "foreign land" have you had to "sing a song of Zion"? How did you manage to do this?

**2.** How has that circumstance(s) enabled you to touch others?

**3.** Who in your life has been an inspiration of "singing God's grace" in times of trial? How does/did that affect you?

***Living Our Realities*** ***Mark 2:23-26***

*One Sabbath he was going through the grainfields, and as they made their way, his disciples began to pluck heads of grain. And the Pharisees were saying to him, "Look, why are they doing what is not lawful on the Sabbath?" And he said to them, "Have you never read what David did, when he was in need and was hungry, he and those who were with him: how he entered the house of God, in the time of Abiathar the high priest, and ate the bread of the Presence, which it is not lawful for any but the priests to eat, and also gave it to those who were with him?"*

In his early days, George Carlin's humor was fresh and brilliant: he had a way of helping us see the folly and humor in our everyday behavior. His routine about the "ritual" we go through when we lose something is a classic. In it, Carlin points out that when we lose something, we continue to go back to where the lost item is "supposed" to be! And we continue to follow the same ritual even though the lost item is no longer in that place! "But that's where it was! That's where I put it! That's where it's *supposed* to be!" And we continue to complain as we ignore the obvious facts.

In the scripture passage above, the Pharisees are annoyed that Jesus allows his followers to perform work on the Sabbath by picking grain. In defending his disciples, Jesus argues from the scriptures that human needs and changing situations take precedence over ritual and custom. He reminds them that when David and his men were fleeing for their lives, they sought food from Ahim'elech the priest (1 Samuel 21:1-6) – and the only bread he had was the holy bread offered in the Temple, which none but the priests were allowed to eat. But he gave it to them due to their hunger, and David and his men ate the sacred bread. The situation had changed, so they acted in a different manner.

How many times in our own lives, or in our parish or work community, do we continue to do the same things as if we expect a different outcome? Our liturgies are dry, but we don't want to change the music. Our work is stressful, but we refuse to delegate or change jobs. Our relationships aren't working, but we refuse to get counseling. We want to find what has been lost, but we continue to look for it in the same place – as if we believe that doing the same thing often enough will somehow produce a different result! When in fact, as one saying puts it: "If you always do what you've always done, you'll always get what you've always gotten."

"Cast your net on the other side of the boat" is still the advice Jesus would give us today!

It's natural for us to want to cling to the familiar, or to live out of our former realities. I know people who lived through the Depression era, and that experience continues to dominate their lives. I know others who have been abused, or gone through a divorce, and continue to live out of that experience, unable or unwilling to try again and trust a new relationship. Like the Pharisees, some even continue to live as if the situation has not changed.

"Have you never read what David did, when he was in need and was hungry?"

David looked at the current reality of his life situation, and had the courage to do something out of the ordinary. He had the courage to do something new and different; something unconventional, something that other people might not understand.

He lived out of current information and present realities, and Jesus did the same.

If we want to change our lives – if we want to find the part of us that has been lost in a sea of expectations and past experiences – then we, too, must do something new and different. We can't keep following the same habits, customs, or rituals; we can't keep living out of the same needs or out-of-date realities. We can't keep looking in the same old places and expect to find something new, or to recover that which has been lost!

Scripture challenges us to live like David, and like Jesus: we are challenged to live out of our *current* realities. We are challenged not to let our habits, rituals, roles, or past experiences define us. Whether it's a religious ritual or simply how we live our everyday lives, we need to constantly ask ourselves what is driving our decisions and behavior.

We need to read and remember what David did, when he was in need and was hungry!

**Reflection:**

**1.** What behavior or attitude do you need to change ? How can you begin to change it?

**2.** What rituals or experiences in your life do you need to challenge in order to live a more authentic life? How can you begin to do so?

**3.** When have you needed to look at a circumstance or event differently, in order to achieve a better result in your life? How did you accomplish that?

***The Sword***

***Exodus 1:8-10***

*Now there arose a new king over Egypt, who did not know Joseph. And he said to his people, "Behold, the people of Israel are too many and too mighty for us. Come, let us deal shrewdly with them, lest they multiply, and, if war breaks out, they join our enemies and fight against us and escape from the land."*

***Matthew 10:34-35***

*Do not think that I have come to bring peace to the earth. I have not come to bring peace, but a sword. For I have come to set a man against his father, and a daughter against her mother, and a daughter-in-law against her mother-in-law.*

*"**I**f it ain't broken – don't fix it!"* During my years as an accountant in the business world, that old saying was not only a phrase I often quoted, it was virtually my mantra for living! In other words, as you travel through life, stay on the main roads. Keep control of your life, and don't take unnecessary chances. On the back roads, there are hills that prevent you from seeing where you're going, and unexpected turns that can disrupt your plans and lead you to roads that aren't even on the map. Avoid them. Be cautious. Be safe.

*"If it ain't broken – don't fix it!"*

The above passage from the Old Testament demonstrates the extremes to which our resistance to change and our need for control can take us. In Genesis, Joseph arrives in Egypt after escaping from the well into which his brothers had cast him (Genesis 37:22). Years later, in the Exodus passage, his descendants are becoming so "numerous and powerful" that the leaders of Egypt grow fearful of losing control, so the

Pharaoh commands that all newborn males be killed. Several centuries later, a similar fear prompts King Herod to seek the death of Jesus by slaughtering the innocent children in Bethlehem and its vicinity (Matthew 2:16).

The above passage from Matthew could make you wonder how Jesus ever got the title "Prince of Peace"! He speaks like a wide-eyed radical, someone you might expect to find preaching and carrying a sign on a street corner. He tells us to leave our families, leave our homes, and leave our dead-end jobs; he asks us to let go of everything that is safe and secure. "For I have come to set a man against his father, a daughter against her mother..."

Our need for security often makes it easy for us to continue doing what we've always done, without giving it a second thought or even being aware of its destructive nature. And as scripture reveals, there is a natural inclination for us to want to eliminate or rid ourselves of those things which challenge us to change, or threaten to take away the illusion of control over our lives. And our quest for safety often goes beyond physical security: we want protection against new ideas, uncomfortable truths, disturbing doubts, and sometimes even honesty.

"If it ain't broken – don't fix it!"

I descended into the hell of depression on the night I finally realized the depths of pain and suffering that my own fears and need for control had caused my family. It finally came home to me that I had destroyed relationships, slaughtered dreams, and dashed untapped potential on the rocks of my own anxieties. Until that moment, I hadn't seen my life as broken, so I saw no need to fix it!

Jesus has a different mantra for us: *"If it ain't broken – break it!"*

Clearly, Jesus didn't come to endorse or enshrine the status quo. He came to break things! *Take the sword that I bring,* I can hear Jesus saying today, *and cut out everything in your life that separates you from me.* Smash the idols you have created. Sever those relationships that are not life-giving, even if it puts you at odds with those you love. Root out the fear that paralyzes you and the anger, addictions, or memories that hold you captive.

Then get off the beaten path, travel some back roads, and let me surprise you! Some of the turns may be painful, but through them, you can grow and become more alive. Through them, you can become more sensitive, more caring, and more fully human. Though them, you can awaken gifts and talents beyond your imagining.

...and keep the sword.

You'll need it again – and again – and again!

**Reflection:**

**1.** What is there in your life that needs to be broken, changed, or released?

**2.** Spiritually, how have you become "more alive" or "more whole" by something that you have changed or "broken" in your life?

**3.** How have you been surprised when you have let go of, given up, or abandoned something that was keeping you from growing in your relationship with God?

***Broken Glass Shining*** ***Acts 8:4-8***

*Now those who had been scattered went about preaching the word. Thus Philip went down to [the] city of Samaria and proclaimed the Messiah to them. With one accord, the crowds paid attention to what was said by Philip when they heard it and saw the signs he was doing. For unclean spirits, crying out in a loud voice, came out of many possessed people, and many paralyzed and crippled people were cured. There was great joy in that city.*

There is a page in my copy of Henri Nouwen's book *Life of the Beloved* that is dog-eared, soiled, and worn; it bears the marks of countless hours of prayer and meditation. On that page, Nouwen recalls a scene from Leonard Bernstein's musical *Mass* (written in memory of President Kennedy): a priest, richly dressed in liturgical vestments, is lifted up by his people. He towers high above the adoring crowd, carrying a glass chalice – but when the human pyramid collapses, the priest falls to the ground and the chalice is shattered. In the next scene, the priest is in a T-shirt and jeans, walking through the debris of his former glory. He gazes upon the fragments of the chalice and mutters, "I never knew... broken glass... could shine so brightly."

It is April 1993. We have two kids in college – and the job I loved is gone, a casualty of misunderstanding, betrayal, and falsehood. I was "asked to resign." (That's the politically correct way of saying it; the phrase doesn't make what happened hurt any less.) I'm not a provider anymore, and my life is out of control. What happens now?

The gospels tell us again and again not to worry about what we can accomplish; we are simply to believe, and God will take care of accomplishing things. In scripture, we get a glimpse of how God gets things done even in our adversity. We see it in this passage from Acts: the new Christians were facing persecution and death. People were running for their lives and "scattering throughout the countryside." But even in that scattering, the gospel was spread, as "those who had been scattered went about preaching the word." As a result, "there was great joy in that city [Samaria]."

As I remember 1993, I marvel at how God manages to get things accomplished. After losing my job, I went back to school and had the privilege of being in college at the same time as my two sons. It's a blessing afforded to very few, and a highlight of my life. And my new Religious Studies degree led to my going to work in the Church. Most days, it was an exciting and rewarding second career – new doors were opened, with possibilities beyond my imagination (not the least of which is this, my third book!).

We are broken, Nouwen reminds us. Broken that we might be blessed (by becoming more sensitive, more open, more fully human), and blessed that we might be given (used by God to bring about his kingdom).

We don't have to accomplish anything, Jesus tells us. All we have to do is believe. Believe that we are clay in God's hands. We are broken pots, to be repaired and renewed by the Potter.

Broken glass, shining brightly.

**Reflection:**

**1.** How has God accomplished something in your life that you could never have imagined?

**2.** When have you seen "broken glass" shine brightly in someone else?

**3.** What experience in your life has made you feel like you were "clay in God's hands"?

## *The Hill Country* *Luke 1:35-40*

*And the angel answered her, "The Holy Spirit will come upon you, and the power of the Most High will overshadow you; therefore the child to be born will be called holy— the Son of God. And behold, your relative Elizabeth in her old age has also conceived a son, and this is the sixth month with her who was called barren. For nothing will be impossible with God." And Mary said, "Behold, I am the servant of the Lord; let it be to me according to your word." And the angel departed from her.*

*In those days Mary arose and went with haste into the hill country, to a town in Judah, and she entered the house of Zechariah and greeted Elizabeth.*

I feel somewhat unqualified to write a reflection on this passage: after all, the story is about the bonding between two pregnant women! And I can think of many who would be more qualified to share a reflection on this topic (such as almost anyone who's been a mother). I have certainly never been pregnant, nor would I ever claim to know the depth of the bond between two women who are sharing that experience.

But I do know something about the "hill country"! It is always a difficult journey, and some choose not to travel that road. But visiting her cousin Elizabeth was important to her, so "Mary traveled to the hill country." The hill country harbors danger and uncertainty, but it is also from such heights that we first see the morning light.

Neither Elizabeth nor Mary expected to be pregnant; scripture tells us that Elizabeth was "too old," and Mary "had not known man." For both women, there were many unanswered questions – yet both women had said "yes" to God. Yes, I will turn over control of my life. Yes, I will trust in you. Yes, I will journey to the hill country, with all of its anxieties and apprehensions. And yes, I will rejoice in the morning light.

Listening requires change, a new direction; listening may require you to redefine yourself. The Lord calls us in our sterility and in our barrenness. If we believe, the Lord will move in our life and make us fruitful in ways we cannot imagine.

Mary was a young woman who had let go of all control and surrendered her life to God. She had not yet lived long; she had not been beaten down, betrayed, or bitterly disappointed. She didn't know the dangers of the "hill country." But she trusted in the promise, and she believed in the power of "visitation moments" to affirm her "yes" and strengthen her faith in what God can do for us – and with us.

There is great power in "visitation moments." There is power in community, in support, and in being with others who believe. Mary and Elizabeth needed each other – to affirm each other's hearing of God's word and their response to it.

This scripture passage, then, invites us to focus on God as the center of our lives. It invites us to live in the joy that comes with surrendering control; it invites us to travel to the hill country, where we may stumble and fall, or become anxious and afraid. It invites us to travel to the place where the light is first seen and darkness is overshadowed.

Will you allow God to lead you there today?

**Reflection:**

**1.** If you have experienced a "visitation moment" in your life, how did it occur and how did it affect you?

**2.** What "morning light" have you experienced when you have allowed God to move in your life in a way you never expected?

**3.** What difficult travels do you face in your life today? Whom can you "visit" to affirm your direction and give you strength?

### *The BE-attitudes* *Matthew 5:1-7*

*Seeing the crowds, he went up on the mountain, and when he sat down, his disciples came to him. And he opened his mouth and taught them, saying: Blessed are the poor in spirit, for theirs is the kingdom of heaven. Blessed are those who mourn, for they shall be comforted. Blessed are the meek, for they shall inherit the earth. Blessed are the merciful, for they shall receive mercy.*

"It's just a job!" my wife said to me, having tired of hearing my complaints about the unfairness of my termination from the company where I had worked for fifteen years. "Stop saying that!" I responded in a loud voice. "It's *who I am!*"

Thankfully, after many years and much counseling, I've been able to move beyond that limited self-image. But I suspect the same attitude has been expressed many times at recent graduation ceremonies and parties: "So what do you want to *be*, now that you're out of school?" The question is right, but the answers are wrong! The answers often betray our societal attitude of equating what we *do* – a doctor, a teacher, an accountant, a computer tech – with who we *are*. My wife still needs to remind me from time to time that we are human "beings," not human "do-ings"! Our culture would have us believe that we must *do* something to have value as a human being – but, as Christians, what we do flows from who we are; it flows from our *be*-ing.

The above scripture passage presents Matthew's version of the Beatitudes (which are also found in Luke's gospel). I find it helpful to think of them as the *BE*-attitudes. These attitudes tell us what we are to *BE* as Christians: we are to be meek and we are to be merciful, thirsting for holiness, and at one with those who mourn. As Christians, we are to adopt an attitude and life of *BE-ing*: being merciful, being kind, being meek. We are to *BE* with each other in sorrow, *BE* able to show mercy, *BE* there when others are hungry. *BE* there for those in prison. *BE* wherever we are called. *BE* in the moment. *BE* there to comfort, to listen, and to love.

Christian life is about *BE-ing* together. Can we *BE* together today? Can we open our hearts to each other? Can we *BE* with those we love – and even those we don't? Can we *BE* with those who frighten us, and those who have hurt us? Can we *BE* with those who forgive us – and even those who don't?

Can we *BE* different than the world around us?

Can we *BE* followers of Jesus?

It's all in our attitude... the *BE*-Attitudes!

**Reflection:**

**1.** In your own life, how are you different than the world around you? Do you think your lifestyle makes a difference in the world? If so, in what way?

**2.** Who in your life do you think exemplifies the beatitudes? How do they live this out?

**3.** What are some of the things you do as a human "BE-ing"?

### *Turning the Tables* *John 2:13-15, 18-20*

*The Passover of the Jews was at hand, and Jesus went up to Jerusalem. In the temple he found those who were selling oxen and sheep and pigeons, and the money-changers sitting there. And making a whip of cords, he drove them all out of the temple, with the sheep and oxen. And he poured out the coins of the money-changers and overturned their tables. So the Jews said to him, "What sign do you show us for doing these things?" Jesus answered them, "Destroy this temple, and in three days I will raise it up." The Jews then said, "It has taken forty-six years to build this temple, and will you raise it up in three days?"*

**I'**m a movie buff. Often, at the end of a long day or a trying week, a movie is my escape mechanism. I especially love to turn up the sound and watch a film that has little "socially-redeeming value," but lots of helicopters and explosions (full enjoyment requires that my wife be out of town or shopping!). One of my favorite movies in this genre is the original "Rambo" film, *First Blood.* Using Green Beret guerrilla tactics, John Rambo (played by Sylvester Stallone, in the famous role that would generate an endless string of sequels) battles and defeats an entire posse of small-town deputies in the woods (yes, "action flicks" are like that). He then warns the local sheriff (played by Brian Dennehy), "Call this thing off or I'll give you a war you won't believe!"

I was reminded of that line as I read this scripture passage! Jesus is nearing the end of his ministry; he's running out of time and getting impatient. He has provided numerous signs and scripture references to establish his authority for what he says and does, and he has just turned over the tables of dishonest money lenders and driven them from the Temple.

And the Pharisees (yet again) ask for a sign of his authority to do this! Jesus is angry. I can imagine him thinking: "You want a sign? I'll give you a sign you won't believe – 'Destroy this temple and in three days I will raise it up!'"

It's a sign they won't believe because the Pharisees take Jesus literally and respond from their preconceived idea of a temple. "It took 46 years to build the Temple," they laugh scornfully, "and you're going to rebuild it in three days?"

St. Paul asks us, "Do you not know that *you* are the temple of God?"

I hear Jesus saying today: invite me into your temple, let me turn over a few tables and drive some things out – and I'll give *you* a sign you won't believe!

Let me turn over that table of security you have worked so hard to build, and sacrificed so many relationships to defend – and let me teach you to trust.

Let me drive out the attitude that defines who you are by what you do – and invite you into a relationship as God's beloved.

Let me overturn that table of "shoulds" and "oughts" – and show you the gifts and talents hidden underneath it.

Let me drive out those resentments... so you can experience forgiveness.

Let me chase away your fears of scarcity... and show you the blessings of abundance.

Let me turn over the table of who you are... and show you who you can *become.*

I can turn an accountant into an author! I can give a fearful person confidence! I can make a timid person bold! My servant Paul said it well: "*You* are God's temple." *You* are my Father's house.

Let me shatter your illusions – and give you hope. Let me destroy your security – and give you faith. Let me take away your independence – and give you grace.

Let me rebuild your temple... and I'll give you a *life* you won't believe!

**Reflection:**

**1.** What does being a "Temple of God" mean to you?

**2.** How might you enable another person to rebuild their life?

**3.** What do you need to do to rebuild the temple of your own life?

***Nets in the Sand*** ***Mark 1:16-20***

*Passing alongside the Sea of Galilee, he saw Simon and Andrew the brother of Simon casting a net into the sea, for they were fishermen. And Jesus said to them, "Follow me, and I will make you become fishers of men." And immediately they left their nets and followed him. And going on a little farther, he saw James the son of Zebedee and John his brother, who were in their boat mending the nets. And immediately he called them, and they left their father Zebedee in the boat with the hired servants and followed him.*

In the above scripture passage, Jesus calls the disciples to follow him and they "leave their nets." What strikes me is how quickly the disciples respond to the invitation – so quickly, in fact, that they apparently left their father sitting in the boat, probably looking like a deer caught in the headlights, wondering what happened! One of my favorite hymns captures the disciples' attitude well: *"All I treasured, I have left in the sand there / Close to you, I will find other seas."*

I suspect there must have been a series of smaller graces that prepared the disciples for that full commitment, that final "yes," that allowed them to "leave their nets." In doing so, they left their way of life – everything they treasured – lying in the sand, and followed Jesus.

The image of "leaving nets lying in the sand" always returns me to that Saturday morning in 1993 when I cleaned out my desk and left my office behind as I prepared to enter college – as a 53-year-old freshman!

This was more than changing jobs: this was letting go of my means of making a living, and changing my self-image. I knew it was a defining moment, but I wasn't sure where I would find those "other seas," or how I would get there.

I often wonder why such transitions have to be so painful. Whether it's a career change, a change in relationships, or a diminishing physical capacity, some part of us must usually be left lying in the sand. The invitation to change, and the openness to find Jesus in that change, often comes in the form of some experience of failure or powerlessness, or of being brought low. Sometimes it takes turmoil, unrest, or heartbreak to force us to let go, so we may be open to God's call for a new direction in our life; sometimes we must feel that pain before we are willing to change directions, leave our nets, and look for other seas. But, as St. Paul reminds us, the redemptive love of God works best in our weakness (2 Corinthians 12:9) – that is, when we have left everything we treasure lying in the sand.

I suspect Jesus saw some deep struggle – some restlessness or lack of peace – in the spirits of the disciples, which told him they were ready to leave their nets. And I suspect that they looked in Jesus' eyes and felt the love that set them free. For it is love that calms our anxiety and gives us the courage to leave our nets – all that we treasure – lying in the sand.

As I move from Autumn into Winter, as with every change in my life, I must ask myself: am I ready to live the song that I sing?

*"All I treasured, I have left in the sand there / Close to you, I will find other seas."*

**Reflection:**

**1.** "To become fishers of men" implies a process. What event(s) in your life have enabled you to become a better follower of Jesus?

**2.** What personal weakness has been a grace that allowed you to be more open to God's invitation?

**3.** What nets will you leave in the sand that you might follow Jesus to other seas in your life?

### *Wretched Food* *Numbers 21:4-5*

*From Mount Hor they set out by the way to the Red Sea, to go around the land of Edom. With their patience worn out by the journey, the people complained against God and Moses, "Why have you brought us up out of Egypt to die in the wilderness? For there is no food and no water, and we loathe this wretched food."*

Sometimes I write for you, the reader. But at other times, I write mostly for me – and you are more or less reading my "journal" as I struggle with the vicissitudes of life. And so it is, as I share this reflection...

Recently, we enjoyed a special time with friends in Ft. Wayne, Indiana. A concert by *The Lettermen* (a popular singing group from the late '50s through the '70s) drew us together; we listened to the music and sang some familiar tunes as we enjoyed the nostalgia of our high school years. It was a delightful occasion.

But when my wife and I came home early to have dinner with friends who were returning from vacation, our anticipation of another joyous time was quickly dampened by sad news: my dear friend's cancer had returned with a vengeance. There were still tests to be run, but the early prognosis was not good.

As I reflected on the above passage, I easily identified with the chosen people in the desert who, "with their patience worn out by the journey... complained against God." They were disgusted with their "wretched food"!

Today I, too, feel worn out by the journey; I am complaining against God. I, too, am disgusted with this "wretched food"! I'm tired of good people being struck down by illness, and their songs ending too soon. We promised our friends: "We will be there for you. We will be where you are, we will not call this curse a blessing, and we will scream with you against the unfairness of it all!"

It's almost certain that none of us will go through life without suffering. Statistics say that half of us will experience a divorce, many will lose a job, and virtually everyone will be treated unfairly in some way. Even when our suffering seems relatively small – not making the team, being rejected by the college of our choice, or failing to land that dream job – it still hurts, and we join with those who have lost loved ones, failed in their marriage, been injured in an accident or afflicted by disease. Together we look over our shoulders to see what disaster is coming next. We've lived long enough to know that it's just a matter of time.

"Let it go," we are often told, "and just move on." But it isn't always that easy. We can learn from our mistakes and grow from our suffering, but we never become a blank slate. Our very identity has been indelibly shaped – marred, sullied, graced, and nourished – by the pains of living.

When Jesus rose from the dead and appeared to his friends, he still bore the wounds of his previous agony; they were not only proof of his resurrection, but of the fact that God was redeeming his suffering and using it to begin a new age. And Jesus "showed himself" to his friends in their time of defeat: he came to them where they were, spoke to their doubt, and walked alongside their dejection.

Christians revere the crucified Jesus because it is his suffering that speaks of the good news! It is his rejection that reveals the truth, his defeat that gives us hope, and his death that brings us life.

Salvation is God's gift to the broken.

We do not proclaim an abstract and unmarred gospel. We are what we are today because yesterday *happened*. So we need not deny our pain, soft-pedal it, or call it something that it isn't. Instead, we proclaim Christ crucified – and the grace that is revealed, and the hope that is found, when our nets are empty.

**Reflection:**

**1.** How do you reclaim hope when you are "worn out" by the journey of life?

**2.** What are some of the "pains of living" that have formed you as a person?

**3.** Is it difficult for you to show yourself (pain, brokenness, suffering) to those in your life? Why or why not?

**_The Third Day_** **_Matthew 12:39-40_**

*But he answered them, "An evil and adulterous generation seeks for a sign, but no sign will be given to it except the sign of the prophet Jonah. For just as Jonah was three days and three nights in the belly of the great fish, so will the Son of Man be three days and three nights in the heart of the earth."*

**I** have written several reflections on the sign of Jonah ... but there is another sign embedded in this scripture passage that is subtle and easily missed. It has to do with Jonah being released from the belly of the great fish on the third day.

In scripture, a lot of things happen on the "third day" – in addition to Jonah being released, Abraham was saved from sacrificing his son when God intervened on the third day, and in the book of Genesis, Joseph freed his brothers from prison on the third day. And, of course, Jesus was raised on the third day.

One is almost compelled to ask: didn't anything ever happen on the second day, or the fourth, or the tenth? Why always the third day?

It's our natural inclination to read scripture with a modern-day mindset, so when we come to a passage that refers to this day or that, we immediately think in chronological terms. But when scholars see multiple uses of a term in scripture, they ask: what's really going on here? What's the deeper meaning of the text?

Scholars tell us that, in scripture, the "third day" is not simply a marking of time, but a theological statement. For example, Hosea (6:1-2) tells us, "He will revive us after two days and on the third day he will raise us up to live in his presence."

And Exodus (19:11) enjoins us to, "Be ready for the third day, for on the third day the Lord will come." So the "third day" is seen as the day of deliverance – it is our assurance that God will not abandon us in times of trial.

But we shouldn't take these words too literally! Scripture doesn't mean that, if I lose my job on Monday, I'll get a new one on Thursday, or that, if my spouse leaves me on Wednesday, he or she will be back by Saturday! But scripture *does* tell us that, no matter what is going on in our life, God will not abandon us; he *will* rescue us. As Christians, we are to live in expectation and await that metaphorical "third day." Of course, we don't know how long the actual in-between time will be, or what may happen while we wait for God to make his presence known; we are simply to trust in him at all times, to wait patiently, and to put our hope in him as our refuge and protector (Psalm 62).

A few years ago, I went for my annual physical and my doctor told me: "Jim, for a guy your age (*he could have left that part out!* I thought), you're in good shape. Just keep working, don't smoke, take your cholesterol medicine, and don't step in front of an oncoming truck – and you should live a long life." Six months later, I was suddenly diagnosed with bladder cancer! And I found myself yelling, "Hey! What happened to 'keep working, don't smoke, and take your cholesterol medicine'?!"

I didn't even see that "truck" coming! And suddenly, I'm thrown into that in-between-time – waiting for the third day.

With the courage of Abraham, I went on: "You see, God, the problem is – I read your book, and I know what happened to your Son as *he* waited for the third day! And, like him, I would just as soon skip that part, if that's okay with you!"

My sister, however, put it this way: "We grow in the valley, not on the mountaintop."

I'm now more convinced then ever that the purpose of our time in the valley is to make us more sensitive, caring, and understanding people. "Valley time" puts us more in touch with ourselves, with God, and with each other. Suddenly, I'm forever connected to every person who has ever heard that dread diagnosis: "It's malignant"! And certainly, my sympathy and compassion for them is sincere.

As I write this, I'm scheduled for my annual exam. I don't know what deliverance will look like for me; I suppose it will either mean the tumor will not return, or I that I will be given the courage to walk in the valley.

But I believe this: no matter what may happen to us in life, God will not abandon us.

*I believe – in the third day!*

**Reflection:**

**1.** What "third day" experience have you had in your life? How did you pray at that time?

**2.** Was there a time when you doubted God's faithfulness in your life?

**3.** Was there a time in which God demonstrated that he did not abandon you?

***Robert*** ***Luke 18:28-30***

*And Peter said, "See, we have left our homes and followed you." And he said to them, "Truly, I say to you, there is no one who has left house or wife or brothers or parents or children, for the sake of the kingdom of God, who will not receive many times more in this time, and in the age to come eternal life."*

**I** sometimes think I'm the Christian for whom God invented the two-by-four!

I share the following story with you so that, when I say I'm slow to recognize Jesus at work in my life and am not very sensitive to hearing his voice, you will have some idea of what God is dealing with when he tries to work with or through me. After all, I'm an accountant, and I've always tried to keep my life in nice, orderly columns.

One of my problems with Jesus is that he doesn't stay in his column! He never looks the way I think he should look, he never acts the way I think he should act, and he never uses the people that I think he should use; no wonder I don't readily see him active in my life. Even in my best moments, when he's gotten my attention (often by using that metaphorical two-by-four!) and I think I understand what's going on, it usually turns out that I'm still clueless. It seems God is always calling me to a deeper level – someplace beyond my established boundaries, or to the outer edges of my comfort zone. My encounter with a man named Robert is a typical example of the extremes to which God must often go to get me to look inward.

In the early 1990s, my wife, Helen, and I took separate vacations for the first time. That's not a comment on our marriage – rather, events just played out that way. She and her sisters planned one of their famous get-away weekends, a tradition which began back when they were young, stay-at-home Moms and needed a break from their routine. So, once a year, my wife and her sisters would get together at an out-of-town location to shop at a new discount store or explore an outlet mall.

This particular year, however, the tradition reflected a significant upgrade: their plan was to rent a condo on a lake in Northern Ohio and power-shop every outlet mall from Upper Sandusky to Cleveland! That venture and "vacation" were irreconcilable terms to me, so I opted for Plan B: my brother and his wife were going to a business convention in San Francisco that same weekend and had invited me to tag along. (Simply comparing the words "San Francisco" and "Upper Sandusky" made the decision an easy one!)

In those days, when my wife and I traveled, we usually bought Traveler's Cheques – but since it was only me this time, I decided not to bother and just took a bunch of fifty-dollar bills with me instead.

The convention my brother was attending ended late Saturday evening, with a farewell dinner to which only attendees and spouses (not brothers) were invited. We all had reservations for a flight out the next day – and since I had no other evening plans, I decided to attend Mass on Saturday evening instead of Sunday morning. From the window of the cable car I rode in, I could see the spires of St. Mary's Church, and I decided to get off at the next stop and attend six o'clock Mass there (which would still leave me time for a bit more sight-seeing on my last night in San Francisco).

Little did I know that the Lord was waiting for me!

St. Mary's is an old historic church supported by large stone pillars. Shortly after I sat down, I realized that I was behind one of those pillars and wouldn't be able to see the altar during Mass, so I quickly changed seats. A few minutes later, a man in old, shabby clothes came in and sat down in the pew in front of me. He had a worn shoulder bag with him, in which he seemed to be carrying all his worldly possessions. He carefully set his bag in the pew.

"There's a tradition at St. Mary's," the celebrant began. "We introduce ourselves to each other before we worship together." With that invitation, the man turned to me. He was not attractive: his hair was matted, he was unshaven, and some of his teeth were missing. But he smiled broadly when I said I was from Indiana, and told me that he had once lived in the town of Peru, Indiana... and that his name was Robert.

As Mass progressed, I decided that, instead of putting money in the collection basket, I would just give it to Robert. *After all,* I thought, *a few bucks will mean a lot more to Robert than it will to the parish.* I felt good about my decision, and a bit proud of my generosity. But the Lord always calls us to a deeper commitment: when I looked in my wallet, all I had there was a fifty-dollar bill! I quickly put my wallet away. *No way! I don't give that much at collection time, even in my* own *parish!*

I turned my attention back to the Mass just as the gospel was being read, and I heard the rich young man ask Jesus: "Lord, what must I do to gain everlasting life?"

*I'd help this poor guy if I could,* I thought. *Heck, I'd even give him twenty bucks – if I could just get change for a fifty!*

In his homily, the priest said, "Most of us aren't called to give up *everything*, but we are called to share what we have by responding to the need of the moment."

*I can't do it!* I protested to myself, hoping I had not actually said it out loud. *That's my last fifty bucks, and it's got to last me three more days!*

"We have another tradition at St. Mary's..." The voice of the celebrant again brought me to attention. "We join hands when we pray the 'Our Father'." I looked around. There was no one else in my pew... but right in front of me was Robert, standing alone with both arms stretched out.

I reached forward and took Robert's hand, and we prayed the "Our Father."

At the sign of peace, Robert turned to me. Instinctively, I wrapped both arms around him and said, "God loves you, Robert!"

And Robert began to cry.

I felt his tears against my cheek as he whispered, "No one... has ever taken my hand... in church before!"

As I turned to offer the sign of peace to the person behind me, Robert was on his knees sobbing to himself. My mind continued to wander: *If I did give him my last fifty, how do I know he wouldn't use it for drugs or something?* So I struck a bargain with God: *if Robert goes to Communion, I'll take it as a sign that he's a good person and give him the fifty dollars.*

At Communion time, Robert was the first one out into the aisle! I stared at his bag, lying on the pew in front of me. And I thought: *This is my last chance... I could just slip the fifty into his bag. I'd love to do that – but I've still got three days of vacation, and how would I get home?*

The thought came to me so loud and clear that it seemed like a voice from heaven: *use your Gold Card!*

Embarrassed, I realized that, yes, I could just use my credit card, or even borrow some money from my brother, and I would be fine. With that thought, I slipped my last fifty-dollar bill into Robert's bag, went to Communion, and left the church immediately afterward so Robert would not be embarrassed when he returned to the pew and discovered what I'd done.

On Sunday, my brother, his wife, and I flew to Los Angeles to visit our sister Fran, as planned.

On Tuesday, we were on the plane heading home, and I was again thinking about Robert. I considered all the events that had to have taken place for our paths to cross. What if I hadn't decided to go to San Francisco? What if I hadn't gone to Mass on Saturday instead of Sunday? What if I hadn't chosen to attend St. Mary's? What if I hadn't changed seats? What if the priest hadn't asked us to introduce ourselves to those around us? All of these things had to happen, I mused, for me to take this man's hand in church for the first time, and tell him that God loves him.

*Is it all just coincidence,* I wondered, *or could God actually be working through me?*

We were somewhere over Missouri when I reached into the overhead compartment to get a book to read – and out of that book fell a fifty-dollar bill!

I sank back into my seat in stunned disbelief. And, as clearly as you are reading these words, it seemed the Lord said to me: *What's the matter, Jim? Didn't you believe me when I said that whatever you give will be returned to you? And, by the way, you still don't get it ...*

*I didn't send you to St. Mary's for Robert – I sent* Robert *there for* you!

**Reflection:**

**1.** How has God worked through you in an unexpected way? What message did you discern from this?

**2.** How has God unexpectedly sent someone to you, to reveal some truth about yourself?

**3.** When was a time you *didn't* reach out to someone when the opportunity presented itself? How did that affect you? What did you learn from the incident?

### *Sign of Jonah* **Luke 11:29-30**

*When the crowds were increasing, he began to say, "This generation is an evil generation. It seeks for a sign, but no sign will be given to it except the sign of Jonah. For as Jonah became a sign to the people of Nineveh, so will the Son of Man be to this generation."*

In this scripture passage, Jesus gets upset (yet again) when the Pharisees ask for a sign. Their desire for a sign is understandable: they simply want to know what's going on! They, like us, want some sense of understanding and control in their life, so they ask questions: "You say you're the Messiah, but how can we be sure? If you are the Promised One, what are you going to do now that you're here? What is this 'new kingdom' you speak of going to look like? What's going to happen to us?"

Those sound like reasonable questions to me!

One of the most difficult things people have to contend with is ambiguity – that is, the randomness and uncertainty of life. We don't like that; we want to know what's going on! We want things to make sense to us, which at least gives us the feeling of being in control. And we especially want this when something bad happens that is beyond our control: we want to know *why* the hurricane destroyed our home, *why* we got cancer, or *why* our loved one was killed in a freak accident.

In order to make sense of life's events, we sometimes try to force explanations: "everything happens for a reason," some will say, or "it's all part of God's plan," or even "you're being tested." But such explanations – true or not – betray our own search for a sign, some kind of confirmation that things are okay or under control. Even the *illusion* of control seems better than accepting the randomness of life! To believe that a person was killed just because they happened to be in the wrong place at the wrong time, or that we get cancer because cells sometimes run amok for no discernable reason, or that a life of poverty is often just an accident of birth, is very unsettling to us.

Jesus has heard it all before! He has provided signs, but they are not good enough for the Pharisees – nor for us! They are not clear or definitive enough; they leave questions unanswered – and we still do not feel in control of events. In the above passage, Jesus gets upset and says to them: "From now on, no sign will be given (to you) except the sign of Jonah!"

The prophet Jonah was sent to Nineveh to preach repentance, since God had vowed to destroy their town if the people of Nineveh did not repent. But Jonah didn't like his assignment, so he tried to escape by going in the opposite direction. And God brought him back – in the belly of a great fish. No doubt Jonah's preaching was half-hearted, and he was clearly anticipating that those sinful people would get what they deserved. But much to Jonah's amazement, the people repent! So God shows mercy and doesn't destroy them.

As he sits in the hot desert sun afterwards, Jonah is upset. I can imagine him mumbling to God: "You brought me all this way, and I don't even get to see one house burn! What's with that? These people committed all kinds of sins, and you just let them get away with it. You drag me here in that big smelly fish, I preach all day in the hot sun – and then you let the sinners go free!" Suddenly, a tree sprouts in the desert and gives Jonah shade. Then Jonah realizes that he did nothing to *earn* the shade; he did nothing to *merit* the tree. It was God's free gift – just as mercy was God's gift to the people of Nineveh.

This is the sign I give you, says Jesus, "the sign of Jonah." A tree sprouting in the desert – an unearned gift, freely given. Abundant grace – forgiveness for the asking, mercy without limit. Love without measure. Salvation, if you accept it.

In this passage, Jesus seems to be saying: let this sign be enough for you.

Let the strength of knowing me and the awareness of my presence carry you through the tough times. I am greater than your sense of control, stronger than the answers you seek! Your house may be gone. Your cancer may be incurable. Your difficult relationship may never be reconciled.

But *I am here* – a tree of grace, sprouting in your desert.

**Reflection:**

**1.** What "sign of Jonah" (mercy, grace, or forgiveness) have you received in your life?

**2.** When have you been a "sign of Jonah" to someone else?

**3.** Do you believe in the randomness of life? Why or why not? How do you see God working in the circumstances of your life?

### *Returning Home*

***John 10:1-4,11***

*"Truly, truly, I say to you, he who does not enter the sheepfold by the door but climbs in by another way, that man is a thief and a robber. But he who enters by the door is the shepherd of the sheep. To him the gatekeeper opens. The sheep hear his voice, and he calls his own sheep by name and leads them out. When he has brought out all his own, he goes before them, and the sheep follow him, for they know his voice. I am the good shepherd. The good shepherd lays down his life for the sheep."*

***Matthew 18:12***

*What do you think? If a man has a hundred sheep, and one of them has gone astray, does he not leave the ninety-nine on the mountains and go in search of the one that went astray?*

"The cow got out!" I ran home as fast as my nine-year-old legs could carry me, shouting the terrible news. To my amazement, my older brother didn't move from the shade in which he was resting. "She'll find her way home at milking time," he assured me. "Then we'll chase her around the fence and she'll go back into the pasture at the same place she got out. That's how you find the hole in the fence." *Wow*, I thought to myself, *my brother is smarter than a cow!*

When Jesus compares us to an animal, I often wish he had chosen a gallant collie or a noble steed... or at least, a cow that has enough sense to find its way home at milking time! But no – Jesus compares us to *sheep*. Sheep don't have enough sense to break out of a pasture, much less find their way back in; they just sort of wander away, without aim or effort. They usually don't even realize that they are away from home or in any danger. On the farm, we couldn't just sit and wait for the straying sheep to come home – we had to go find them and bring them back. (Hmm... maybe Jesus was onto something there!)

As Christians, most of us don't break out of the pasture; we don't purposely set out on a road of selfishness and sin. We are like sheep: we just sort of wander away. We wander away from loved ones... we just don't make the effort to stay in touch anymore. We avoid meaningful relationships... they take too much time and effort, and we don't want to take the risk or make the commitment. We don't mean to hurt anyone as we grasp for money and possessions... we just want to feel safe and secure. We usually don't even realize that we have left home or lost our way. We don't recognize our need for God's grace.

When we wander off, Jesus doesn't just lament the loss or assume that we'll eventually find our way back. No, the Good Shepherd goes *searching* for his sheep until they are found! We are in exile – a voice crying out in the desert – and Jesus the Good Shepherd is crying out for *us*, hoping that we will hear his voice and return home.

In a sense, I "return home" when my concern is for the *other* sheep; I return home when I can hear the voice of others who are crying out in the desert. I return home when I can hear the voice of those who have lost a loved one, or who have lost a job. I return home when I can hear the cry of those who are hungry, and those who are alone.

I return home when I *become* the shepherd.

To hear the voices of others, I must learn to listen – and to recognize that's it's not all about me! I am not at home when I respond to someone's pain with easy catch phrases like "I know what you mean," and think that I have heard their story.

I am not at home when I say "that's nothing; listen to this," and distance myself from someone by topping their story with one of my own. Rather, I must hear them, see their suffering, and allow them to share their pain. To hear the voice of another, I must step close to them. I must taste the salt of their tears, and feel the burden of their bitterness.

I cannot chase these sheep around the pasture with doctrines, definitions, or sound bites and try to force them to come back. Rather, I must be at home in *their* desert, and let *them* cry out. I must let them cry out from the depth of their struggles, wanderings, sadness, and grief. I must be content to listen with love, and stare into eyes that cannot see back, until that day when *"Every valley is filled / And every mountain made low / And we can say to the city of Judah / Here is your God."*

Your God is the Good Shepherd. Your God is called Emmanuel, "God-with-us."

Come, Lord Jesus!

**Reflection:**

**1.** In what way/s have you experienced God as a Good Shepherd in your life?

**2.** Is there some way in which you have "wandered away" from the voice of the Good Shepherd in your life? How might you find your way back?

**3.** What can you do to hear more clearly, and to recognize the voice of the Good Shepherd? What can you do to be a "good shepherd" to another?

***The Signs*** ***John 6:23-26***

*Other boats from Tiberias came near the place where they had eaten the bread after the Lord had given thanks. So when the crowd saw that Jesus was not there, nor his disciples, they themselves got into the boats and went to Capernaum, seeking Jesus. When they found him on the other side of the sea, they said to him, "Rabbi, when did you come here?" Jesus answered them, "Amen, amen, I say to you, you are looking for me not because you saw signs but because you ate the loaves and were filled."*

***S**ynoptic* ("seeing together") is a term that is often used in reference to the gospels of Matthew, Mark, and Luke. These three writers tell basically the same story of Jesus in basically the same sequence, so the term is used to refer to them collectively. In the synoptic gospels, Jesus chastises the Pharisees for repeatedly asking for a sign to prove that he is the Messiah, because their goal is to discredit him (Mark 8:11 and Luke 11:29 are examples).

In John's gospel, from which the above passage comes, the word "sign" is synonymous with "miracle." In that context, there are seven signs, or miracle stories, in John's gospel (which are told to confirm the divinity of Jesus): changing water to wine (2:1-12), the healing of the official's son (4:43-54), the healing of a paralyzed man (5:1-15), feeding the 5000 (6:1-15), walking on water (6:16-24), the healing of a man born blind (9:1-12), and raising Lazarus from the dead (11:1-44).

It is to these signs – or miracles – that Jesus would have us look today.

I have attended my share of prayer meetings and retreats, and have heard many proclaim that, when they prayed or "gave their heart to Jesus," their business was saved, their illness was cured, or they got the job they wanted. And, if that's the case, I'm happy for them. But I often feel like I'm in the back of the church, and I want to scream: "Hey, wait! I prayed for her health, and my sister still died of cancer! I gave my heart to Jesus, and I still lost my job!" And I hear Jesus asking us: *do you believe in me because you are successful? Do you believe in me because you have a good life? Do you believe in me because you prayed and got what you wanted?*

*Do you believe in me because you "ate the loaves and were filled"?*

I'm much more touched by the young witness in my prayer group who said: "I'm an alcoholic... and I still struggle with that every day." I believe – because I *am* the miracle. I'm the one who is leaning on Jesus as I try to walk. I'm the one who was blind, but is now beginning to see. I'm the one who was dead and is being raised to life again!

We are reminded by this scripture passage that we should not be looking for Jesus in the easy answers of a "free lunch," but in the ongoing *challenge* of his miracles. We should look for him in the seeming hopelessness of an unemployment line, and believe that, somewhere out there among all those "noes," there is a "yes." We should look for him in the despair of a doctor's waiting room, and say with my young co-worker "I have cancer – cancer does not have me!" And maybe we can even say, with my (now not-so-young) retreat brother, "I'm the one being raised!"

During Autumn and in all seasons, remember to look for Jesus in the signs!

**Reflection:**

**1.** Have you ever prayed for a miracle and not received it? In your mind, how did you reconcile asking and not receiving?

**2.** To what in your life have you been "blind and could not see"?

**3.** What are your thoughts when someone attributes success, good fortune or receiving a miracle to praying or "giving their heart to Jesus"?

**4.** Do you believe God answers prayers? If so, why do you think he answers some and not others?

## *A Little Red Wagon* *Matthew 5:38-40*

*"You have heard that it was said, 'An eye for an eye and a tooth for a tooth.' But I say to you, Do not resist the one who is evil. But if anyone slaps you on the right cheek, turn to him the other also. And if someone steals your coat, give them your cloak as well."*

**A** literal reading of this scripture passage can paint a rather unappealing picture of what is expected of us as Christians: the passage seems to say that we are to submit to abuse and let people steal our stuff! In the proper context, however, this passage can be seen as a challenge to us to take charge of the situation and force our opponents to re-examine their actions.

In the time of Jesus, an offended superior would slap a servant or a slave with the back of his hand (on the subordinate's right cheek). But if the person was a social equal, he would be slapped with an open hand (on the recipient's left cheek).

So, the "right cheek" in this passage is an important distinction. If someone strikes you on your right cheek (thus treating you as a slave and not acknowledging your worth), then "turn the other cheek" – and make them re-examine their actions. They must either acknowledge you as an equal by slapping you on the left cheek (with their open hand), or stop the violence and not strike you at all!

The Mosaic law of "an eye for an eye and a tooth for a tooth" that Jesus quotes in the above passage may seem harsh to us, but it was an improvement over the practices it was intended to replace. In an age of personal revenge, massacres, and blood feuds, the Mosaic law raised the level of response to one of fairness: the punishment had to fit the crime.

But Jesus raised the standard even higher: "If someone steals your coat, give them your cloak as well!"

"The wheels of the wagon are gone!" My sister ran into the house shouting the news, and several of us hurried outside and stared in disbelief. Our "Red Ryder" wagon was more than just a favorite toy; it was also an important means by which we children could reduce Mom's workload on the farm. We often used it to haul water, carry wood, or perform other chores; whenever something was too heavy for us to carry, we could always "put it in the wagon and pull it." We considered that little wagon a vital piece of equipment.

"J. C. Fletcher [the local delinquent] was here yesterday and I'm sure he took the wheels," my sister Dot reported. My siblings and I immediately went in to "Mosaic Law mode": "Well, let's go steal something of his!" I was about eight years old, and I couldn't believe Mom's response: "The Bible says that, if someone steals your coat, you should give them your cloak as well! So take the rest of the wagon and go give it to Mrs. Fletcher."

With tears in our eyes, my brother Paul, sister Fran, and I carried the remains of our precious wagon through the field, over the creek, and down the road to our neighbor's house. Once there, we reluctantly repeated our rehearsed lines to Mrs. Fletcher: "We know J. C. already has the wheels, so we'd like to give him our wagon." Choking back our sobs, we set the wagon in the yard and went home. The next morning, our wagon – its wheels re-attached – was back in our yard!

As I waited for my turn to take a ride in our restored vehicle, I muttered, "I guess that Bible stuff really works..." "Remember that!" Mom whispered.

"Remembering that" – whether it's a prayer clearly answered, an event that turned out right, or a path that led to new growth – continues to be a source of strength for me in difficult times.

Thanks, Mom!

**Reflection:**

**1.** What words do you remember from long ago that still guide you?

**2.** Have you ever had the opportunity to cause someone who was offending you to re-examine their actions? If so, what was the outcome?

**3.** How can you go beyond a hurtful situation and "give your cloak" to the offender?

***Return to Slavery*** ***Galatians 5:1,4-5***

*For freedom Christ has set us free; stand firm therefore, and do not submit again to a yoke of slavery. You are severed from Christ, you who would be justified by the law; you have fallen away from grace. For through the Spirit, by faith, we ourselves eagerly wait for the hope of righteousness.*

"You're going to Egypt?" my friend asked me excitedly. "I have a friend in Cairo; you'll really like him!" So, to make a long story short, my friend's friend and I connected through Facebook and we spent a day together.

Ossama was surprised by my interest in Islam and the Koran (Qur'an), and I readily expressed the dissonance I perceived between the friendliness and tolerance I was experiencing in Egypt, and the harsh image of Islam we often get from terrorists or other extremist groups. On his iPod, Ossama quickly showed me passages in the Koran which state that the most harshly condemned are those who do evil in the name of Allah. And he eagerly showed me passages in the Koran that are similar to those which appear in our Christian scriptures. He took special delight in pointing out that Jesus (whom Islam views as a holy prophet, along with Abraham, Moses, and other Biblical figures) is mentioned more times in the Koran than Mohammad!

But I was saddened by his response when I asked how, according to Islamic belief, people are saved. His answer could have been taken straight out of my experience of the pre-Vatican Catholic Church, in which rules were meant to be strictly followed and everything was counted, weighed, and measured. That experience created for me an image of a judgmental God – a policeman in the sky – and that image had haunted and frightened me for many years.

I was Ossama's guest, so the time wasn't right – but I wanted to tell my new friend about grace! I wanted to share with him the "good news" of salvation! And I wanted to share with him my resolve that I would never again submit to the legalistic "yoke of slavery" he was describing . I know something of that yoke; I lived under its weight for much of my life! It takes many forms, and all of them have the power to render God's presence in us invisible to others – and most especially, to ourselves.

This invisibility, I've learned (after many painful years), only happens when we *allow* it happen. It happens when we give someone else power over us: when we let them define who or what we are, or when we accept their definition of what gives us value. Sometimes we give society that power over us, or the boss or company we work for, or even the church where we worship. We may give that power to our spouse or a parent, or we may allow it to be dictated by the conditions in which we live. For example, society tells us pretty clearly: "You are what you do, and your value is in the wealth and possessions you own." If we accept that premise (as I did for so many years), we submit to a kind of slavery – because then what gives us value (a job or possessions) can be taken away, and our sense of value as a person along with it. Wearing a yoke of slavery such as this gives someone else the power to destroy our identity, diminish our true value, and render us invisible.

But Jesus says that knowing the truth shall set us free! (John 8:32)

To be "visible," a counselor once told me, we must become like an old tree which is *valued for itself*. The tree's value is not in what it can become (a piece of furniture, say, or firewood) or even what it can potentially do (give someone shade); its value is in simply *being a tree,* and doing that which makes it a tree – standing tall and sturdy, and being stately and beautiful.

Similarly, *our* true value is in simply being human – as God made us – and doing that which makes us human. And the only thing we must "do" for our wholeness is to become *more fully human.* We must become more sensitive, more loving, more kind, more understanding toward others – as Jesus calls us to be – and therefore more visible to one another and to ourselves.

Will you let the truth set *you* free?

How will you seek to become more visible today?

**Reflection:**

**1.** How has society's message "you are what you do, and your value is in your wealth and possessions" affected you? How have you tried *not* to let it affect you?

**2.** Against what slavery must you stand firm so the real you – the "God-in-you" – can become more visible?

**3.** In what area do you need to become more "fully human"? How might you work toward that goal?

### *Not Only My Feet, Lord* *John 13:4-9*

*[Jesus] rose from supper. He laid aside his outer garments, and taking a towel, tied it around his waist. Then he poured water into a basin and began to wash the disciples' feet and to wipe them with the towel that was wrapped around him. He came to Simon Peter, who said to him, "Lord, do you wash my feet?" Jesus answered him, "What I am doing you do not understand now, but afterward you will understand." Peter said to him, "You shall never wash my feet." Jesus answered him, "If I do not wash you, you have no part with me." Simon Peter said to him, "Not only my feet, Lord, but also my hands and my head as well!"*

It's interesting that, in St. John's gospel, we are not told of the institution of the Eucharist, a ritual so central to our Christian faith. Rather, John has Jesus show us how we *become* Eucharist. To become the bread we eat at the table of the Lord, to become Jesus in our world – we must serve, and become the slave of all!

The washing of feet was a common practice of hospitality in the time of Jesus – and understandably so, given the filth-strewn dirt roads of first-century Palestine, in which animals commonly traveled and most people walked barefoot or wearing sandals – but it was work reserved for slaves. Yet, as the apostles sit down to supper, Jesus takes a towel, wraps it around his waist, and begins to wash their feet!

It's difficult for us to understand the full impact this must have had on the apostles. To them, it was the most undignified thing Jesus could have done – it would be like the President of the United States scrubbing the toilet, or the Pope emptying a bedpan. The apostles are aghast: "What is he doing?!" Then

Jesus comes to Peter, and Peter says: "No! You will not wash my feet! I will not let you degrade yourself this way!"

Jesus is exasperated. I hear him saying: "Peter, Peter... this is my last hour, and still you do not understand. Unless you become like a slave – unless you live to serve the needs of others – you cannot *be* my disciple."

And Peter, perhaps for the first time, begins to truly understand what it means to serve in God's kingdom. And he commits himself fully: "Then... not only my feet, Lord, but my hands and my head as well."

Our call to serve is usually not a dramatic one; there are no thunderbolts to knock us from our horse, no burning bush. We are simply called to serve in the duty of the moment. Our call can be as unexciting as an alarm clock in the morning or as common as a child's cry at night. It can be the voice of the man who begs a quarter from us on the street, or the groan of an elderly woman who needs help with the supermarket door. It could be the call of a charity solicitor, the plea of an annoying relative who craves our support, or perhaps just the whisper of a sad friend who wants someone to listen.

But whatever it may be, when our call comes, may we surrender in God's service and make ours the prayer of Peter: *"Not only my feet, Lord, but my hands and my head as well."*

**Reflection:**

**1.** The call to serve is lived out in many ways. How are you living out your call to serve in your daily life?

**2.** Who do you know who is an inspiration to you in living out of the call to serve?

**3.** How might being a good receiver of service also be an act of serving?

## *The Third Chapter:*

# Believe His Word

*"And since He bids me seek His face,*
*Believe His Word and trust His grace,*
*I'll cast on Him my every care,*
*And wait for thee, sweet hour of prayer"!*

*Sweet Hour of Prayer*
*William W. Walford, 1845*

### *Everything to God in Prayer*

***Romans 12:12-15***

*Rejoice in hope, be patient in tribulation, be constant in prayer. Contribute to the needs of the saints and seek to show hospitality. Bless those who persecute you; bless and do not curse them. Rejoice with those who rejoice, weep with those who weep.*

**M**y mother died more than fifteen years ago, but I can still hear her humming an old Baptist hymn from her childhood as she worked around the farmhouse: *"Oh what peace we often forfeit / Oh what useless pain we bear / All because we do not carry / Everything to God in prayer."*

Mom took *everything* to God in prayer. As a single parent struggling to raise seven kids on a broken-down old farm, with few resources and cut off from neighbors by distance and lack of transportation, she often had nowhere else to turn.

Mom prayed with expectation – she simply expected God to do what he had said he would do! It was an oft-repeated scene at our house: no money, no food, and no way to get to town to get anything. One day, when I was about ten years old, I was crying because I was hungry and feared there would be nothing for us to eat. I remember Mom putting her arm around me and saying, "Don't cry, son. Jesus fed five thousand people – and there are only eight of us!"

I am now in the Autumn of my years, and I have faced many of life's problems: job loss, sickness, the worry parents have for their children, and the death of loved ones. It's usually after I have exhausted all of my own efforts and have nowhere else to turn that I think about Mom's faith, and I remember the hymn: *"Oh what peace we often forfeit / Oh what useless pain we bear / All because we do not carry / Everything to God in prayer."*

I don't pray much differently now than I did in earlier times: I still pray *for things,* even though I fully realize that this is not the highest form of prayer. I still pray for the needs of those I love, as well as for my own health and well-being. But I do turn to God more quickly these days, as I realize that I have less and less control over matters.

Still, I find that the more difficult part of Mom's advice is not to *take* everything *to* God in prayer – but to *leave* everything *with* God in prayer! Yet, as Jesus says: which of us, by worrying, can add a single hour to our life? (Luke 12:25) And he therefore counsels us to simply trust in God for all our needs.

Trust means that we pray our questions, not our answers. And we must accept that grace rarely follows *our* prayers or *our* plans.

Living in the Autumn of my years, I find that I more quickly move into the spirit of that other Baptist hymn that Mom would sometimes sing... I more readily let go of my need for answers and am content to simply "believe his word and trust his grace!"

**Reflection:**

**1.** How do you pray for the things you want or need?

**2.** Does taking things to God in prayer make a difference in your life? How?

**3.** Is it easier for you to trust in God's grace now that it was years ago? Why or why not?

### *Follow Me* *Mark 2:13-15*

*He went out again beside the sea, and all the crowd was coming to him, and he was teaching them. And as he passed by, he saw Levi the son of Alphaeus sitting at the tax booth, and he said to him, "Follow me." And he rose and followed him. And as he reclined at table in his house, many tax collectors and sinners were reclining with Jesus and his disciples, for there were many who followed him.*

"I haven't cleaned a bathroom or vacuumed a floor in twenty years," my wife Helen bragged to a group of her hospice co-workers at dinner one evening. "My husband does those things!" I reveled in the *ooohhhs* and *aaahhhs* and took the appropriate number of bows, but I also felt a need to explain. When Helen started nursing school, I became "Mr. Mom" and took over many of the housecleaning chores so she would have more time to study. I foolishly assumed that, when she graduated, she would reclaim those duties – but, as she said that evening, it's been twenty years... and I'm beginning to think it's not going to happen!

A few months ago, it was our turn to host our faith-sharing group, and I was busy cleaning the house when my vacuum cleaner died. So I did the "guy thing" and went online to find a replacement. I explored websites, got a sense of the market, and found the perfect vacuum: state-of-the-art filtration, on-board tools, the right price – and enough power to suck up half of Cleveland! However, I learned at the store that it had to be "put on order" and our group was coming over *that night*, so the overriding issue became availability. Under those circumstances, it didn't have to be the "perfect" vacuum – it just had to be available immediately. I could make any brand work.

I've often wondered why Jesus chose such an unlikely group to be his disciples: fishermen, tax collectors, self-seekers, doubters – in some ways, the dregs of society. But I think Jesus' choice of disciples may have been much like my purchase of a vacuum cleaner: availability mattered more than perfection. If Simon and Andrew were willing to leave their nets and follow him, Jesus could make them into something more. If they weren't available – if they were not willing to follow him – then it wouldn't matter how qualified or capable they were. Availability mattered more than perfection. Jesus can make any brand work!

The one who is available – the one who says "yes" and follows through – is the one who makes a difference. You can train someone to lead or serve effectively, but you can't train a "yes"; willingness arises from faith and character. Look at the motley crew that Jesus assembled: sinners, outcasts, the flawed, and the broken – in other words, people like us. And this rag-tag entourage changed the world.

In my experience, the ideal leader, servant, or colleague is the one who is willing enough to try, humble enough to learn, brave enough to fail, foolish enough to imagine a better world, and faithful enough to join hands with the flawed and broken.

Jesus isn't looking for someone who is perfect – he's looking for someone who's *available*. He's looking for someone who will immediately leave their nets and follow him. Let the more qualified wave their credentials; let the "perfect" and more capable claim their "higher calling." But Jesus knew what we know: nothing happens if we're not available. Nothing happens until we say *yes!*

How will you say "yes" to Jesus today?

**Reflection:**

**1.** Describe a time when you have been called to "leave your nets" to say "yes" to God's call. Did you do so? Why or why not?

**2.** Have you ever felt "not good enough" or "not perfect enough" to allow yourself to be used by God? How were you able to put those feeling aside and say yes to him?

**3.** How can you make yourself available to do the work that Jesus might call you to do?

### *God Praying* **Luke 7:11-15**

*Soon afterward he went to a town called Nain, and his disciples and a great crowd went with him. As he drew near to the gate of the town, behold, a man who had died was being carried out, the only son of his mother, and she was a widow, and a considerable crowd from the town was with her. And when the Lord saw her, he had compassion on her and said to her, "Do not weep." Then he came up and touched the bier, and the bearers stood still. And he said, "Young man, I say to you, arise." And the dead man sat up and began to speak, and Jesus gave him to his mother.*

**S**oft music is playing in the church, and a burning candle reminds us of God's presence. Our connectedness is felt as we take each other's hands in prayer: "... for my brother who is serving overseas, keep him safe, O Lord." "That my friend who has been diagnosed with cancer will be returned to health, we pray to you, O Lord." "Father, comfort and console those who grieve the death of a loved one this night..."

All our prayers have been expressed and now we stand in uncomfortable silence. In an almost inaudible voice, our retreat director breaks the silence, "And what do you think is God's prayer for you tonight?"

The question hangs in the air. God's prayer for *me?!* I never imagined *God* praying!

The woman in the gospel passage above could have stepped out of today's headlines! She has lost everything: first her husband, and now her only son is dead! Jesus is moved with compassion. He cuts through the "red tape" of his Jewish culture, in which contact with a dead body makes a person ritually impure. He touches the young man's body and restores him to life – and then he "gave him back to his mother." It's a touching scene, and restoring life seems to be so easy and natural for Jesus. So easy, in fact, that one might ask: why doesn't he do this for everyone? Why did he choose to restore this woman's son, and not another's? What about all those other people who are suffering the loss of a loved one? Why doesn't Jesus restore them, too?

As believers, we face the same question today, in our own world! How do we explain the crushed homes and flooded streets when a tidal wave occurs? How do we explain the deaths of the innocent, or why their prayers to be spared seem to go unanswered? Those who see God as being in control of all things may wonder why this town was destroyed, and not another. They may see a disaster as some kind of test, or a message from the Lord. Others may wonder if their faith is too weak, and if that is why their prayers are not answered. Some will blame God for allowing – if not causing – such suffering. Others will seek to defend God through rationalization, and still others will question the value of prayer.

I think one of the reasons that Jesus didn't heal everyone was because he wanted us to see the bigger picture. He wanted us to understand that *we* play a vital part in how this world operates. "*You* give them something to eat," he answers in Matthew 14:16, when the disciples tell him that the people are hungry. And Jesus seems to be saying to us: "*You* heal them. *You* comfort and console them. *You* restore them to life. You have seen what I do – and I tell you that you will do even greater things!" (John 14:12).

We ask for Jesus' help; we pray for a miracle… and God gives us each other.

Faith isn't about analysis; it isn't about answering the 'whys.' Faith is about call and response, come and see, stop and help, take the cup, hear the cry, enter Jerusalem. Don't wait for someone else, or some guarantee of success – just do it!

Faith sees the storm and doesn't try to explain it away. Faith sees the hurricane coming and says, "If I suffer tonight, Lord, let me see your hand in the hand of my neighbor who comes to help. And if I am kept safe, let me be that neighbor to another."

Faith isn't about changing the laws of nature; it's about changing what is in our hearts. Faith isn't about re-writing our fate; it's about writing new songs for our souls. Faith is about new sight. Faith is about turning to the wounded, and finding the strength to serve. Faith doesn't explain things; faith submits to what is. And in all circumstances, faith looks for opportunities to love and serve.

People sometimes wonder where God is in the midst of tragedy. When tragedy strikes, God is the first one on the scene! God is the first response team! God is praying for us! God is rooting for us! God is cheering us on: "Yes! That's the way! You can do it!"

You can help. You can heal. You can restore life. You can bring hope.

You don't need a miracle.

You can *be* the miracle.

**Reflection:**

**1.** How has someone been a miracle to you? How have you been a miracle to someone else?

**2.** In the midst of personal hardship or tragedy, how do you pray? And for what do you pray?

**3.** In what circumstances of your life have you experienced God's "prayer" for you?

**_Casting Stones_** **_John 8:3-7_**

*The scribes and the Pharisees brought a woman who had been caught in adultery, and placing her in the midst they said to him, "Teacher, this woman has been caught in the act of adultery. Now in the Law Moses commanded us to stone such women. So what do you say?" This they said to test him, that they might have some charge to bring against him. Jesus bent down and wrote with his finger on the ground. And as they continued to ask him, he stood up and said to them, "Let him who is without sin among you be the first to throw a stone at her."*

**I** can never read this passage without thinking of my friend John. John was the "old man" at the office back when I was a "thirty-something." It's easy to be judgmental at an age when you still think you have most of life's answers – and when John thought we "young bucks" were being judgmental during a conversation, he would simply lay a small stone on the table without comment. Eventually someone would ask: "What's that, John?" And John, in his deepest growling voice, would say: "That's the stone for the one of you who is without sin to cast!" His little routine reminded us of our own imperfections – and the tone of the conversation always changed.

I think the reason we are reminded so often in scripture not to judge others is that passing judgment sets us above another person, and can blind us to our own sins, shortcomings, and imperfections. Perhaps this is why Jesus warns us not to try removing the speck from another's eye while there is still a log in our own! (Matthew 7:3-5)

Not being judgmental, however, does not mean we must tolerate unacceptable behavior. And in this scripture passage, Jesus provides us with a model for handling such situations.

Jesus doesn't pass judgment on the woman caught in adultery – he doesn't even pass judgment on those who are about to kill her! They were, after all, acting within the law (under ancient Jewish law, adultery was a sin punishable by death). So he leaves the decision of how to act up to the individual (metaphorically, that would be us). In effect, he says: *go ahead and throw your stones, if you're OK with that! But let me ask you something first: are you without sin? And before you throw a stone, you might want to think about this...* and then he begins to write in the sand. We don't know what he writes, but whatever it is it causes the readers to look inward... and suddenly, they lose their taste for dealing out judgment and punishment. They become less self-righteous, and more tolerant and forgiving.

Acknowledgement of our own sinfulness unites us all.

"My name is Jim – and I am a sinner." With those words, I introduced myself to the people of St. Monica Parish as their Business Manager and Pastoral Associate in 1995. And why not? After all, it is the awareness of how much we have been forgiven that makes it possible for us to lay down the stones we would otherwise cast at others. And when we lay down our stones, we are set free! When we lay down our stones, we are no longer plagued by hatred, bitterness, and the desire for revenge. When we lay down our stones, those who have wronged us no longer have power over us. When we lay down our stones, we are open to receive the forgiveness that is ours, and to accept the grace that saves us. And, in our thankfulness for God's grace, we can forgive all injuries and lay down even the heaviest stones we carry.

And surprisingly, we often find that the heaviest stones we hold, the ones that are the most destructive and the most difficult to lay down, are those we cast at *ourselves!* That's why Jesus would have us look inward – for unless we recognize our own faults, and acknowledge our dependence on God's grace, we cannot forgive ourselves... and so, we cannot forgive others.

What stones is Jesus calling you to lay down today, so that you may forgive and be forgiven?

**Reflection:**

**1.** Was there a time when you made a judgment about someone, only to later realize that the judgment was more about you than it was about the other person?

**2.** How do you handle the situation when you see another person being judgmental? How might you handle it differently, or better?

**3.** What imperfection in you might be the cause of your being judgmental of others? What can you do to change or improve those imperfections?

### *Can You See Jesus?* *Luke 19:1-4*

*He entered Jericho and was passing through. And there was a man named Zacchaeus. He was a chief tax collector and was rich. And he was seeking to see who Jesus was, but on account of the crowd he could not, because he was small of stature. So he ran on ahead and climbed up into a sycamore tree to see him, for he was about to pass that way.*

Zacchaeus was a publicly-known sinner: a tax collector. In Jesus' time, local tax collectors earned their income by assessing more tax than was actually owed and pocketing the difference – and they usually made sure it was substantial. With the power of Rome behind them, they could get away with this, but most people despised them and treated them as outcasts. Zacchaeus was a chief tax collector and had amassed great wealth at the expense of others; he was likely hated by many. But anyone who takes the job of tax collector obviously doesn't care what people think of them! No doubt wealthy Zacchaeus was dressed in fine clothes as he waited in the crowd. But he doesn't care what people think, or how silly he looks, as he scrambles up a tree in his fine clothes to see Jesus.

I wonder what called Jesus' attention to that little fellow hidden among the branches and leaves of a sycamore tree? I can imagine some people, from the safety of the crowd, taunting and mocking the unpopular tax collector: "Hey, little man, can you see Jesus now?" But Zacchaeus was willing to ignore what others might think or say – so he could see Jesus!

What about you? What are you willing to do so you can see Jesus?

Are you willing to open your hands and let go of some of your money or possessions to help those in need?

*Can you see Jesus in the other-centered space your giving has created?*

Are you willing to offer your hand and look into the eyes of a homeless person?

*Can you see Jesus in the eyes that look back at you?*

Are you willing to take the first step in reconciling a relationship, admitting your fault, and asking forgiveness?

*Can you see Jesus in the hand you have extended? Or in the hand that receives it?*

Are you willing to spend time with someone who is alone?

*Can you see Jesus in the new friend you have made?*

Are you willing to look deep inside yourself and let go of the resentments, anger, and hurts of your past?

*Can you see Jesus in the new person you have become?*

Like Zacchaeus, are you willing to climb higher, despite everything – to see Jesus?

**Reflection:**

**1.** In what ways do you need to "climb higher" in your life to deepen your relationship with Jesus?

**2.** In what ways do you need to "climb higher" to deepen your relationships with others?

**3.** Give an example of someone you know, or know of, who has followed the example of Zacchaeus. What did they do to "climb higher" so they could see Jesus?

## *Mulberry Trees* **Luke 17:5-6**

*The apostles said to the Lord, "Increase our faith!" And the Lord said, "If you had faith like a grain of mustard seed, you could say to this mulberry tree, 'Be uprooted and planted in the sea,' and it would obey you."*

When I was a kid growing up on the farm in Northern Indiana, we hated mulberry trees. You could eat blackberries, strawberries, and blueberries – but mulberries were useless. We had a mulberry tree in our yard, right where we liked to play and run barefoot. And, on the farm, there was only one thing worse to feel oozing between your toes than fallen mulberries!

Before I started first grade, my father was taken from our family and committed to a state mental hospital. When I was about twelve years old, I found a Bible in his desk and began reading it each day; it somehow seemed to put me in touch with him. This habit of reading the Bible developed into a lifelong interest in scripture.

I remember being elated when I first read this passage: "If you had faith the size of a mustard seed, you could say to this mulberry tree, 'Be uprooted and planted in the sea,' and it would obey you."

Wow! As a kid, I thought it would be really cool to make that mulberry tree move out of our yard and into the cow pasture! It would certainly impress my siblings and gain me favor with Mom – and the Bible said I would be able to do it! So all afternoon and into the night I prayed, and repeated my belief that, in the morning, our mulberry tree would be banished into the cow pasture. The next morning I ran to the window – only to find the tree standing defiantly in the yard.

That experience taught me not to take scripture too literally. In this passage, Jesus is not telling us how to clear away unwanted timber – he is trying to express the power of faith. He is reminding us that faith is the key to removing obstacles and overcoming difficulties in our lives. The "mulberry trees" are those challenges and difficulties we encounter that seem beyond our power to handle.

As I anticipate another post-surgery cancer check-up, I feel a bit like that kid again, praying for the mulberry tree to be gone. I know there are those who believe that if the mulberry tree isn't moved, your faith isn't strong enough, or your prayers aren't persistent enough. But I've also lived long enough to know that faith isn't about controlling God or getting God to do our bidding.

One day, my sister Fran climbed that mulberry tree and yelled down with delight: "Hey, you can see the horizon from up here!"

For me, faith is learning to live with the mulberry tree in the yard – and perhaps climbing it to see a new horizon.

**Reflection:**

**1.** What does it mean to you to have faith?

**2.** When did faith enable you to "see a new horizon" in your life?

**3.** What can you do to strengthen your faith?

## *Gather Into Barns* *Luke 12:15-20*

*And he said to them, "Take care, and be on your guard against all covetousness, for one's life does not consist in the abundance of his possessions." And he told them a parable, saying, "The land of a rich man produced plentifully, and he thought to himself, 'What shall I do, for I have nowhere to store my crops?' And he said, 'I will do this: I will tear down my barns and build larger ones, and there I will store all my grain and my goods. And I will say to my soul, Soul, you have ample goods laid up for many years; relax, eat, drink, be merry.' But God said to him, 'Fool! This night your life is required of you, and the things you have prepared, whose will they be?'"*

You don't have to paraphrase very much to see that the story in this scripture passage is *our* story – indeed, it could be torn from today's headlines!

In the story, a man has worked hard all his life. The passage says that his land "produced plentiful crops" – and anyone who has ever planted so much as a garden knows that you can't get good crops from the drought-ridden farmlands of Palestine without hard work! So this man got his money the old-fashioned way: he earned it! And now he is tearing down his barns and building larger ones to store his harvest and provide for his family's future. One night he puts his arm around his wife and says, "Honey, we've got it made. The kids are out of college, the stock market is up, and I'm only two years away from retirement. We have money in the bank, nice cars, and a condo in Florida. We've realized the American dream!" Then a voice comes from heaven and says: "You fool, this night your life is required of you!"

Like so many of us, the man in this gospel passage attributes everything he has to himself. He refers to *my* harvest, *my* barns, *my* goods. And he says, "I have blessings in reserve for years to come. I'll relax, eat heartily, drink well, and enjoy myself." He puts all of his security in what *he* has built, and thinks he is in control of his life!

"*You fool! This night your life is required of you!*"

How many of us, during the good years, have allowed our possessions, our savings, our stock portfolios, our jobs, our relationships, our personal plans, or our goals to define us? "You are what you do" and "you are what you have" are societal values that most of us, to some degree or another, have adopted – consciously or not. We stockpile wealth and belongings, and take comfort in the barns we have built. Our careers enrich us, the gates around our community protect us, and our savings and possessions give us hope for a prosperous life.

*Foolish person! This night the life you have created will be demanded of you!*

For many of us, the recent economic recession has wrought havoc: the lives we have created are gone, our jobs have been lost – our barns have burned. Our illusions of control have been shattered, and suddenly we are living in fearful and uncertain times.

One day, little Johnny's teacher revealed some frightening news: "The world is round," she said, "and not flat, as we had always believed." On his way home, Johnny shares the shocking news with the first person he meets: "The world is round!" he exclaims. "Impossible," replies the stranger. "Look at the horizon; you can see the edge of the world from here.

Besides, if the world were round, we would all fall off!" Unconvinced, Johnny runs home, still shouting his fear and uncertainty: "Mommy! Mommy! The world is round!" To which his mother calmly replies: "Can you still *love* in a round world?"

Can you still love in a world that is different than you once believed? Can you still love in a world that is not of your making? Can you still love in a world that is not spinning according to your plans?

Can you still love in a round world?

Can you still love when your barns are gone?

**Reflection:**

**1.** In fearful and uncertain times, how is it possible to continue to love and believe? What enables you to do so?

**2.** Do you think it is wrong to live the good life, or to desire it? Why or why not?

**3.** What can you do to diminish the importance of possessions, status, etc., in your life?

**Recognition** **Matthew 13:54-57**

*And coming to his hometown he taught them in their synagogue, so that they were astonished, and said, "Where did this man get this wisdom and these mighty works? Is not this the carpenter's son? Is not his mother called Mary? And are not his brothers James and Joseph and Simon and Judas? And are not all his sisters with us? Where then did this man get all these things?" And they took offense at him. But Jesus said to them, "A prophet is not without honor except in his native land."*

I had been with the company for about ten years when a woman named LeeAnn was hired in a lateral position as Division Controller. I had been instrumental in bringing the company "off the kitchen table" and introducing automation: gone were the days when we tracked receivables on 3x5 cards, hand-wrote checks, and typed our financial reports manually. And gone were the ten- and twelve-hour days, and the half-day-on-Saturday routine. We didn't have to collect the coin laundry money to meet payroll anymore; we were financially stable and had a presence in eight states. Those were the "Camelot years" of that company – when we shared a common goal and called everyone by their first name, and no one had to watch their back.

About six months after she was hired, LeeAnn showed me a memo written by one of the senior partners, which read in part: "LeeAnn, implement the new procedure and tell the other Controller to do the same." Excuse me, the "other Controller"?! When did I become the "other Controller"? The new kid on the block had become the favored one, and I was given "no honor in my native land." And it hurt. This was *my* turf, and I wanted to be recognized!

We've all had the experience of not being recognized, or not being chosen. Most of us have been passed over for inclusion at one time or another: maybe it was a pick-up basketball game, a varsity team, a prom court, or a date with that special someone. Or maybe it was a job promotion, a professional title, or a place on a committee or in a ministry. Rejection hurts, and that sting stays with us for a long time – especially if we felt more qualified than the person who was chosen over us. It hurts when "Teflon Ted" wins again, or "Sandbag Sam" gets another plaque, or the new boss fires everyone and brings in his own team. But the "prophet in his native land" rejections hurt most of all.

Jesus knew the same rejection, and surely felt that pain as he wept over Jerusalem. He knew rejection when the hometown crowd took offense at him, and (according to Luke's account) tried to throw him off a cliff. And he knew rejection when only one of his followers answered his question, "Who do you say that I am?"

As usual, there are parallels in scripture to our own life situations. When Jesus chose his disciples (his "inside group"), he only chose twelve – and we know that Jesus had many other followers, which means that a lot of qualified people got passed over. We know the names of two of them: Joseph called Barsabbas (surnamed Justus) and Matthias. Since they were the two considered to replace Judas, we can assume they were considered qualified – yet they were not initially chosen to be amongst the twelve. And poor Barsabbas became an "also ran" a second time when the lot fell to Matthias instead of him (Acts 1:23-26).

Barsabbas and Matthias provide good role models for us in these situations. We know they continued to serve the Lord, and that personal glory was not their motive. They were passed over at the initial choosing of the apostles as Jesus called forth the disenfranchised – the tax collectors, the doubters, the self-seekers, and betrayers, the less qualified – and left them standing!

Yet both of these men remained committed to working for Jesus in whatever capacity was available, with or without recognition.

What about you? Can you forget that coveted position of honor, and be content to serve faithfully and humbly in the mission? Can you work all day in the vineyard and not envy those who are chosen at the last hour, but are paid the same?

Can you continue to serve, trusting that the Holy Spirit can move more powerfully through you in your current situation than in any other scenario you can imagine?

**Reflection:**

**1.** When have you felt like "a prophet in his native land"? How did you see God working in that situation?

**2.** How might you be able to help someone else who has been rejected, left out, or overlooked?

**3.** When was a time that you felt envious of another because they received what you wanted or deserved? How did you come to terms with those feelings? What did you learn from the experience?

### *Benefit of the Doubt*

***1 Samuel 16:10-12***

*And Jesse made seven of his sons pass before Samuel. And Samuel said to Jesse, "The Lord has not chosen these." Then Samuel said to Jesse, "Are all your sons here?" And he said, "There remains yet the youngest, but behold, he is keeping the sheep." And Samuel said to Jesse, "Send and get him, for we will not sit down till he comes here." And he sent and brought him in. Now he was ruddy and had beautiful eyes and was handsome. And the Lord said, "Arise, anoint him, for this is he."*

***Matthew 12:8-10***

*"He went on from there and entered their synagogue. And a man was there with a withered hand. And they asked him, 'Is it lawful to heal on the Sabbath?'– so that they might accuse him."*

**W**illiam Proxmire, the one-time senator from Wisconsin, got a lot of publicity (and laughs) by exposing governmental waste: $500.00 for a hammer, $4.00 for an aspirin – that sort of thing. His classic case was the government's multimillion-dollar study to determine why kids fall off bicycles. The study concluded that it's because kids "lose their balance"! We laughed and shook our heads at the stupidity of that study: "C'mon – we all knew that!"

But my philosopher son wasn't laughing. He pointed out that we always need to challenge what we think we know. For thousands of years, he reminded me, everyone assumed that a larger, heavier rock would fall faster than a smaller, lighter one. It was a given – everyone knew that – until Galileo dropped two rocks from a tower and disproved what everyone "knew."

We like certainty. We like being right and knowing the answers; it gives us the illusion of control over our lives and makes us feel comfortable. The problem is that when we "know" something, we aren't open to further learning and growth!

There is a familiar story in the book of Samuel: the prophet Samuel is asked to choose the next king. It's a simple job, because Samuel "knows" the qualifications – but Samuel keeps picking the wrong person! God has to keep telling him, "Not that one!"

Samuel keeps making the wrong choice because he is only looking at the outside of the person, and only in the present situation! It is God who reads our hearts and sees our potential. So it is God who guides Samuel to the correct choice: the hidden one, the one out tending the sheep – the one who is youngest and most distant. The one least likely to be chosen.

In this passage from Matthew's gospel, the Pharisees "know" the law: you don't work on the Sabbath. Everyone knows that – it's a given; it's literally the word of God! But they are so fixated on what they "know" that they completely miss the larger *intent* of the law. So when Jesus is about to perform an act of compassion and cure a man's withered hand, the Pharisees object, missing the *meaning* of the law. The Sabbath is part of God's Law, which commands that we do what is right and good – so one can and *must* do what is right and good on the Sabbath! Jesus therefore affirms that it *is* lawful to do good deeds in "violation" of Sabbath restrictions.

We like certainty; it makes us feel warm and comfortable. Yet these scripture passages tell us to stop, think, and act carefully. Doubt can actually be a remarkable grace! God puts doubt into the mind of Samuel to prevent him from choosing the wrong king. And Jesus puts doubt in the minds of the Pharisees to invite them to reinterpret the law and understand more deeply what the Sabbath means.

When we experience doubt as a means to greater insight rather than as a threat, it can be a positive influence. When we doubt our first impressions, we may take the time to look more closely and learn something new. When we doubt what is on the surface, we may look deeper and see people differently. When we doubt what we "know," it can open our hearts to new knowledge and experiences. When we doubt our own motivations and the "rightness" of our actions, we may change how we act toward others.

How will you give yourself – and someone else – the "benefit of the doubt" today?

**Reflection:**

**1.** What doubts have you experienced in your faith, or in your life? How did you deal with them?

**2.** Have you learned something new or gained a new insight by doubting something you always believed? What was it?

**3.** What do you doubt about your faith, your church, or your long-held beliefs? What can those doubts teach you?

### *I'm God and You're Not* **1 Samuel 3:6-7**

*And the Lord called again, "Samuel!" and Samuel arose and went to Eli and said, "Here I am, for you called me." But he said, "I did not call, my son; lie down again." Now Samuel did not yet know the Lord, and the word of the Lord had not yet been revealed to him.*

**I** sometimes get irritated with people who claim to have a pipeline to God. They say they hear God speaking to them in a very clear voice on a regular basis, and they claim to get specific instructions for their life. Maybe I'm just envious, because I tend to relate more to Samuel in this story. Samuel isn't sure that it's God's voice he hears; twice he assumes it is Eli's. It doesn't even occur to Samuel that God would call *him* – after all, Eli the priest is right there! I can relate to that: why would God use me? I'm an accountant, for goodness sake!

In the early days of *Saturday Night Live*, Chevy Chase would open the show with a classic line: "Good evening! I'm Chevy Chase, and you're not!" Why would you use an accountant, Lord, when there are so many others more qualified? I can hear the answer: "Because I'm God, and you're not!"

The awareness that God can use anyone he chooses came to me one day in the early 1980s. I had developed a scripture program that presented the Catholic and mainline Christian approach to scripture interpretation, and I presented it in many parishes. I didn't think of it as a ministry – it didn't occur to me that God might be at work; it was just something educational that I enjoyed doing.

A couple of years into it, I was invited to a parish where everything went wrong. No one had told the Pastor that I was to do a promotion at Sunday Mass – there were no committee members there to introduce me, and there was no sign-up table. I faked it and made it through, but decided that the whole thing wasn't fun anymore and resolved never to do the program again.

During the third of my weekly presentations there, some members of a scripture study group came to me. They told me that one of their members, an elderly lady named Opel, had really been struggling with what I was saying about God. She came from a fundamentalist background, and her experience of God was one of legalism and fear. She told their group that during the course of my program, for the first time in her life, she had come to know God as a loving Father. "That's really nice," I said. "I'd like to meet this lady!" "You can't," came the reply. "Opel died last night."

I was overwhelmed. I had a long, loud talk with God on the way home that night! "What are you doing, Lord?!" I yelled. "I was only having fun, and you send someone like her to me! Didn't you see those guys in black? They're priests! You're supposed to use them. Don't you know that I'm an accountant?!" "Jim," I perceived God to say, "I'm God, and you're not! I can use anybody I want, even an accountant. Even you!"

It is clear that, for whatever reason, God chooses very ordinary people to bring about his kingdom. Remember Peter's response when he was first called: "Depart from me, Lord, for I am a sinful man!" (Luke 5:8) Depart, nothing! Believe it or not, Pete, you're going to lead the charge!

Do you believe that God can use anybody... even you?

How will you let him use you today?

**Reflection:**

**1.** In what event or circumstances did you feel that God was using you to do his work?

**2.** How do you discern what God is calling you to do?

**3.** What do you do if God seems to be silent in your life?

***Eye of a Needle*** ***Matthew 19:23-26***

*Then Jesus said to his disciples, "Amen, I say to you, it will be hard for one who is rich to enter the kingdom of heaven. Again I say to you, it is easier for a camel to pass through the eye of a needle than for one who is rich to enter the kingdom of God." When the disciples heard this, they were greatly astonished and said, "Who then can be saved?" Jesus looked at them and said, "For human beings this is impossible, but for God all things are possible."*

**S**cholars differ as to the meaning of the "eye of a needle" to which Jesus refers in this passage from Matthew. I favor the interpretation that says Jesus is using hyperbole when he speaks of passing through the eye of a needle – that he doesn't mean it literally. Rather, he is using an exaggeration to suggest that one could sooner pass a camel through that tiny opening than one could get a rich man to enter God's kingdom. Others point out that, in the time of Jesus, there was a low, narrow gateway into the city of Jerusalem called "the eye of the needle," which was designed to slow visitors' entry into the city. It functioned something like an airport's security checkpoint: it facilitated crowd control and protected against armed attack. This gateway, it is sometimes suggested, is what Jesus is referring to in this passage; it is difficult, but not impossible, to pass a camel through it. But, to pass through the eye of the needle, the camel's rider had to dismount and unburden himself and his camel of all goods, wealth, and possessions. One couldn't pass through that narrow gateway carrying a bunch of "stuff"! Those who were unwilling to let go and so unburden themselves could not pass through the gateway and enter the city. In either interpretation, Jesus seems to be implying that it is the rich person's greed and selfish desire for wealth that keeps him from entering the kingdom of God.

To capture monkeys in Africa, I'm told, the native people attach a small cage to a tree. The cage is just big enough to hold a banana. The monkey reaches through the bars and grabs the banana, but when the monkey tries to withdraw his prize, the banana won't fit through the bars and the monkey is trapped! Ironically, all the monkey has to do to escape is open his hand and let go of the banana. Let go of his possession. Let go of his greed. Let go of that which holds him captive.

In the same way, Jesus suggests that to pass through the eye of the needle and enter God's kingdom, all we have to do is open our hands! All we have to do is let go of the banana! Let go of our possessions, our greed, our selfishness. Let go of those things that hinder our growth. Let go of those things that hold us captive. Let go of all those things that keep us away from God.

To what are you clinging today? What is it that holds you captive? What keeps you from entering God's kingdom?

Jesus says, "With God, all things are possible." So, with God, you can let go of those things. With God, you can open your hands. With God, you can pass through the eye of a needle!

With God, you can enter the kingdom!

**Reflection:**

**1.** What do you need to let go of to come to the fullness of life and "enter the kingdom"?

**2.** How do you go about "letting go"?

**3.** Tell about something that you have been able to let go of in your life. How did letting go change you?

### *Mending Our Nets* *Matthew 4:18-22*

*While walking by the Sea of Galilee, he saw two brothers, Simon (who is called Peter) and Andrew his brother, casting a net into the sea, for they were fishermen. And he said to them, "Follow me, and I will make you fishers of men." Immediately they left their nets and followed him. And going on from there he saw two other brothers, James the son of Zebedee and John his brother, in the boat with Zebedee their father, mending their nets, and he called them. Immediately they left the boat and their father and followed him.*

"That's kind of a tacky gift," I remarked to my wife one Christmas. It was the fourth or fifth consecutive year that I had received a Christmas tree ornament with the year engraved on it: 1983... 1984... 1985. The ornaments were given as tokens of appreciation for my work in the parish by our then-Director of Religious Education, and they seemed pretty cheap at the time. But we've kept those ornaments for more than twenty years – and again this year, at the annual Christmas party of our mutual friends, I told my (now retired) DRE friend how precious those "tacky gifts" have become to us.

As we decorate our tree each Christmas, we seem to re-live every one of those years. And a swallow of wine usually precedes my hanging of our 1987 ornament: that was the year I got fired on my fifteenth anniversary as the CFO of a local company. And there are other things that took place in 1987 that I'd rather forget...

About ten years ago, our decorated tree fell over and many of our special ornaments were broken, but – you guessed it! – that 1987 ornament survived intact. Perhaps God doesn't want me to forget how busy I was "mending my nets" that year... and how oblivious I was to everything else around me.

It's only in looking back that I see 1987 as a turning point in my life. At the time, I was in my comfort zone, doing my job, avoiding risks, and protecting my family – making sure the nets would hold. And I would have been perfectly happy to mend those same nets until retirement. When it all came apart that year, I didn't see Jesus walking on the shore and inviting me to follow him. And the only thing I did "immediately" was try to put my life back together.

It seems I'm much better at mending nets than I am at following Jesus!

Years passed; there were other setbacks, and another job loss. The nets weren't holding. "You don't need another job," my counselor told me, "you need a life!"

When I entered college at fifty-three to get my Religious Studies degree, I told the Registrar that I intended to go into parish work and stay there "until the Lord calls me home." And it never felt so right, working in St. Monica Parish after I graduated. Soon I was mending the nets again, re-building that world where I'm in control. But times change, priorities change, new visions emerge – and nets break. (Or is it just a new calling?)

After much agony and stress (I don't accept change easily!), I again feel that I am where I'm meant to be: working part-time, writing books, helping parishes become faith-sharing communities, and enjoying speaking engagements. But it's different now, because I see a pattern, and perhaps the message is beginning to sink in: *God never stops calling us.* He doesn't want us to mend our nets – he wants us to leave them in the sand and follow him.

It sometimes takes an experience of failure or powerlessness, or an experience of being brought low, for us to hear Jesus inviting us to stop "mending our nets." The trials, wounds, or sins that leave us raw, exposed, or numb can often become the graces that prepare us for that invitation, and enable us to "immediately" follow him.

I'm writing this reflection on New Year's Day, which is a time of looking back and looking forward. I'm not setting any lofty goals for the new year... but I hope I can more readily stop mending my nets when I'm called to do so, regardless of how the next call might come. Maybe I can draw strength from reflecting on that "tacky" gift, and see a life journey that has always led to higher ground, new growth, and a clearer vision.

And maybe I can move a little more quickly next time, when that figure walking on the shore says "follow me."

**Reflection:**

**1.** What does it mean to say "God never stops calling us"?

**2.** What event or change has led to a turning point in your life? How did it affect you? Did you see it as a call from God? Why or why not?

### *Our Daily Bread* *Mark 8:14-20*

*Now they had forgotten to bring bread, and they had only one loaf with them in the boat. And he cautioned them, saying, "Watch out; beware of the leaven of the Pharisees and the leaven of Herod." And they began discussing with one another the fact that they had no bread. And Jesus, aware of this, said to them, "Why are you discussing the fact that you have no bread? Do you not yet perceive or understand? Are your hearts hardened? Having eyes do you not see, and having ears do you not hear? And do you not remember? When I broke the five loaves for the five thousand, how many baskets full of broken pieces did you take up?" They said to him, "Twelve." "And the seven for the four thousand, how many baskets full of broken pieces did you take up?" And they said to him, "Seven."*

"My father was 63 years old when I was born!"

That's one of my favorite lines to tell at parties, and it always gets a gasp. Then I continue: "...and I have a brother five years younger than I am!"

When I was a child, it wasn't that I thought of my Dad as old... he really *was* old! But I can still see him kneeling on the bare kitchen floor as we said our nightly prayers; I can still feel the warmth of our wood-burning stove, and I can see his gray hair glowing in the dim light of the kerosene lamp. As a five-year-old, the litany of memorized prayers seemed endless as we waited for Dad to end the session with his personal prayer: "O Lord, give us our daily bread, and take care of our children."

Mark's gospel is the oldest of the canonical gospels (written about 65—70CE); it is sometimes called the "pre-Easter" gospel because the original version (which ends at Mark 16:8) contains no sightings of the risen Lord. It also portrays the apostles as being very human: we are told again and again that they "didn't understand." In Mark's gospel, the apostles just don't seem to grasp what Jesus is all about.

In the above passage, when Jesus warns against the "leaven of the Pharisees," the disciples immediately think he's talking about food! They don't get it. Jesus has to remind them that he's not talking about bread; dinner isn't a problem for a guy who previously fed four thousand people! He wants them to understand that there are more important things to be concerned about. "How many loaves were there?" he asks them. "Five." "And how many fish?" "Two." "Do you not yet understand?" Five plus two equals seven! (In Hebrew numerology, the number seven symbolizes perfection.) "And how many baskets were left over?" "Twelve." "Do you not yet understand?" Twelve tribes, twelve of you! (Multiples of twelve symbolize all the people of God.)

Jesus seems to be saying: I have provided the perfect meal, and there is enough to feed all of God's people. So don't be preoccupied with such mundane things as bread! There are greater things that need your attention, and they have nothing to do with lunch! "Beware of the leaven of the Pharisees and the leaven of Herod." (To the ancient Hebrews, leaven was a symbol of evil.) Beware of the "bread" that corrupts; beware of those things that can kill your soul!

The disciples miss what Jesus is saying because they are not present to him in the moment. They had forgotten the bread and were concerned about what they were going to eat; their focus was on the future. But every great spiritual leader in every time and culture counsels us to *live in the present moment!*

The past is gone, and the future has yet to come; *now* is all we ever really have – yet we spend so little time there!

Jesus warns us throughout the gospels: "Stay awake! Be alert! You know not the hour! Worrying will not add a single hour to your life." Yet we still spend most of our time focusing on our past experiences, or being concerned about our future. No wonder we – like the disciples – miss the present moment!

In times of crisis, however, we are forced to deal with reality – and we quickly learn that we can *only* cope with the present. "How are you dealing with the death of your wife?" I asked a friend recently. "One day at a time," was his response. "Sometimes one *hour* at a time."

Life teaches us that we can only live in the present; we cannot live in the past or the future because, for us, they do not exist.

*Now* is all there is.

My father chose the words of his prayer carefully, and I think Jesus chose the words of his prayer carefully too: "Give us *this day* our daily bread!"

Try to observe, this day, how much time you spend concerning yourself with the past, or the future. And when you notice that you are focusing on a time that does not exist, gently call yourself back into the present moment...

...because that's where God is!

**Reflection:**

**1.** What value, if any, do you see to living in the present moment?

**2.** Tell about a time of crisis in your life when you felt that all you could do was to live in the moment.

**3.** How difficult is it for you to live in the present moment? What pulls you away either into the past or into the future?

***It's a Ghost!*** ***Matthew 14:22-26***

*Immediately he made the disciples get into the boat and go before him to the other side, while he dismissed the crowds. When evening came, he was there alone, but the boat by this time was a long way from the land, beaten by the waves, for the wind was against them. And in the fourth watch of the night he came to them, walking on the sea. But when the disciples saw him walking on the sea, they were terrified, and said, "It is a ghost!"*

"It's a ghost!" the apostles shout as they see Jesus coming toward them, walking on the water. And, in a way, I suspect that they *hoped* it was a ghost instead of Jesus! They had all betrayed him by deserting him in his time of need; Peter even had denied knowing him. A visit from Jesus would surely cause them some embarrassment and discomfort!

Hey, I hope it's a ghost too! Because if it's Jesus I see coming, I know he'll ask me to do something that I'd rather not do – like step out of *my* boat. We are all challenged from time to time to leave our comfort zones, to stretch, to color outside the lines... to get out of our boat. We are challenged to do that which seems impossible – to walk on water!

So why do we hesitate to step out of our boat? Marianne Williamson wrote some lines that Nelson Mandela quoted in his 1994 presidential acceptance speech, which put a different spin on the question. (Parenthetical comments are mine.)

*"Our deepest fear is not that we are inadequate."*
(that we *can't* walk on water)

*"Our deepest fear is that we are powerful beyond measure."*
(that we *can* walk on water – that we can do things that seem impossible)

*"It is our light, not our darkness, that most frightens us."* (The darkness of our status quo isn't what frightens us; we are quite comfortable there. What frightens us is what may be asked of us if we make that first step into the light by using our untapped gifts or our hidden talents. What frightens us is how we may have to change our life!)

*"We ask ourselves, "Who am I to be brilliant, gorgeous, talented and fabulous?"*
(Who am *I* to walk on water?)

"Actually, who are you not to be?" Williamson continues. You are a child of God! Your "playing small" (by staying in your boat) doesn't serve the world; there is nothing enlightened about shrinking so that other people won't feel insecure around you! Instead, we are each to make manifest the glory of God that is within us.

And the glory of God is a believer stepping out of the boat!

I don't think Jesus is just chastising Peter when he says, "Oh, you of little faith, why did you doubt?" I think Jesus is also looking past Peter to the disciples still in the boat (that would be us!) and saying, "Oh, you of little faith – why haven't *you* stepped out?"

It's worse than we feared! It's not a ghost we see... it's Jesus, walking on the water – and inviting us to do the same!

**Reflection:**

**1.** When in your life have you "stepped out of the boat"? What were the results?

**2.** Which is more difficult to overcome in your life; the fear of being inadequate or the fear of being "powerful beyond measure"? Why?

**3.** Tell about someone whom you admire for taking the risk and "stepping out of the boat".

***Your Plan Follows Us*** ***Luke 1:30-37***

*Then the angel said to her, "Do not be afraid, Mary, for you have found favor with God. Behold, you will conceive in your womb and bear a son, and you shall name him Jesus. He will be great and will be called Son of the Most High, and the Lord God will give him the throne of David his father, and he will rule over the house of Jacob forever, and of his kingdom there will be no end." But Mary said to the angel, "How can this be, since I have no relations with a man?" And the angel said to her in reply, "The Holy Spirit will come upon you, and the power of the Most High will overshadow you. Therefore the child to be born will be called holy, the Son of God. And behold, Elizabeth, your relative, has also conceived a son in her old age, and this is the sixth month for her who was called barren; for nothing will be impossible for God."*

**I'**m not going to admit my age, but I find myself identifying with Elizabeth and Zechariah rather than Mary and Joseph these days! Did you notice that, when Mary questioned the angel in this passage, she was consoled and given assurance – but in the preceding passages, when Zechariah asked a question ("How am I to know this?"), he was struck dumb? (Luke 1:18-20)

Ok, bad choice of words for Zack – you never want to tick off an angel! But who could blame him for doubting? Mary is young (scholars think she was about fifteen years old), and God hasn't asked much of her yet. She's excited: a new baby, a special calling from God – she can't wait to tell her cousin! On the other hand, Zechariah was called by God years ago and now he's retired. He's "been there, done that." He has paid his dues.

Scripture tells us that Elizabeth and Zechariah are "righteous in the eyes of God, observing all the commandments and ordinances of the Lord blamelessly." They have spent their lives saying yes to God. They have also spent years praying for a child, but Elizabeth was barren and everyone knew it. The once-young couple was now old, and the long wait had become resignation. Sadness creased their faces, as years passed and they accepted their situation. They could see the emptiness in each other's eyes. They have made adjustments and finally accepted what cannot be changed: they will grow old alone.

Now the angel speaks: Listen! God has a message for you. No wonder Zechariah has a question! Listen? Didn't we already answer your call? Didn't we accept our fate? Haven't we paid our dues? But the angel says: God doesn't want you to accept – he wants you to *listen!* Listen again, as in your youth. Listen with excitement, with anticipation, without doubting. It is easier for you to accept than to listen – because listening to God requires change, a new direction; listening to God requires you to redefine yourself – again. Despite your age, despite your previous faith, you haven't yet heard *this* message! You haven't been there, done that! You haven't yet been where I'm going to take you; you haven't done before what I'm going to ask of you.

Give us ears to hear you, O Lord, because our sight fails and we cannot see where you will take us. Remind us again: your plan doesn't call for mere acceptance, nor for surrender. Your plan calls for an eager spirit, an open mind, and an attentive heart. Your plan follows us into darkness; your plan accompanies us into barrenness. Your plan follows us to places we think you do not dwell.

Like dreams of our youth – you call us still.

**Reflection:**

**1.** What do you do to make listening to God a priority in your life?

**2.** Tell about a time in your life when listening to God called you to do something that was surprising to you.

**3.** What do you do when it seems you are not hearing God's call in your life?

### *Hemorrhage* *Matthew 9:20-22*

*And behold, a woman suffering hemorrhages for twelve years came up behind him and touched the fringe of his garment, for she said to herself, "If I only touch the tassel of his cloak, I will be made well." Jesus turned, and seeing her he said, "Take heart, daughter; your faith has made you well."* (New American translation)

"Word choice is the most important element in composition," my creative writing instructor would often say. The process begins with deciding what response you want from your reader. For example, those translations which render the above scripture passage as "the hem of his garment" rather than "the tassel of his cloak" suggest to me an image of a more approachable Jesus. The word "tassel" tends to evoke the image of someone with status or authority – such as a robed king or a bishop – rather than an everyday person.

"Hemorrhage" is another key word choice in this passage. If we move beyond the physical meaning, it evokes a feeling of weariness, of "pouring oneself out" for others. It suggests the depression or sadness that wears away the joy of life as we empty ourselves in the give, give, give situations we often encounter in our daily living. It can also express the unspeakable pain of a traumatic loss.

"What's going on?" I asked my secretary one morning. I had been drawn out of my office by groans and screams coming from behind the closed door of the Pastor's office. I was informed that a hysterical woman had come into the office with a desperate need to talk to someone. She had been arguing with her teenage daughter as they were driving to school that morning and, in anger, the young girl had jumped out of the moving car and been killed when she hit the pavement. This poor mother hemorrhaged her pain for what seemed like an eternity; it literally gave chills to those of us in the outer office. Some even had to leave the room.

We found out later that this woman was not a parishioner; she was not even a Christian – she had just stopped at the first church she saw along the road. Like the desperate woman in the scripture passage above, she just needed to get to Jesus.

As a child, I once heard my mother hemorrhaging her pain when she received a letter informing her of the death of her youngest sister. Mom knew it was financially and physically impossible for her to attend her sister's funeral, or to visit those who shared her loss – and she felt overwhelmed with anguish and sorrow.

For years, I envied my friend's success in business and the financial freedom he was able to provide for his wife and family. But now I see pain hemorrhaging in their eyes as he slips into early Alzheimers', and they watch their dream of enjoying their golden years together slip away.

How can we endure the hemorrhaging pain in our lives, whatever form it may take? Today's passage seems to tell us that we must find a way to get to Jesus! We must find a way to connect with him. It may be through the healing embrace of a friend, a word of scripture, a deepened prayer life, or simply the tenacity to carry our cross.

When we hemorrhage, we too reach out with the desperation of the woman in this scripture passage: can you see her hand tremble as she reaches, and is knocked aside by the jostling crowd? She reaches again, but he's too far away; again and again she reaches, until her fingers finally touch the rough, dusty hem of his garment. It's just enough – the slightest brush... but it is enough.

If we are to survive the hemorrhaging experiences of our lives, we too must find a way to get to Jesus and touch the hem of his garment.

How will you reach out to him today?

**Reflection:**

**1.** Tell about a time when you felt the need to "get to Jesus." What had caused you to feel this way?

**2.** Tell about a time when you were able to *be* Jesus for someone in pain. What did you do for them?

**3.** What attributes of Jesus do you think prompted the woman to seek healing from him? How do we cultivate those attributes in ourselves?

## *Cry Out in Your Desert* *Isaiah 40:3,6*

*A voice cries out: In the desert prepare the way of the LORD! Make straight in the wasteland a highway for our God! ... A voice says, "Cry out!"*

"What do you want the most from the Advent and Christmas season?"

This question was the focus of our prayer group's meeting. My friend's reply was almost inaudible: "I just want it to be over." She then shared her childhood experience of being locked in a closet for thirty days; her only human contact was when food was slid under the door. She explained that, as a result, she didn't feel joy and happiness at this time of year, and societal expectations of those things only exacerbated her pain. Our eyes met, our hands touched; I wanted the holidays to be over too.

The summer was long and hot the year I got my first job: crawling across our neighbor's onion fields, pulling weeds with my siblings. He paid each of us the same rate as our age, so I was making seven cents an hour, and Mom had said it would be our Christmas money. The neighbor said he couldn't pay us until the crop came in, but we didn't mind. The pages of our Sears catalog were smudged and worn from repeated reading, as we each dreamed of getting that special toy we always wanted. This year, Christmas would be different: it would be *good*. But, as summer turned into fall, the excuses began: the crop wasn't very successful, prices were down... besides, the kids hadn't worked all that hard. Finally, Mom had to say the unthinkable – our neighbor would not be paying us for our summer's work. We would not be able to order anything from the Sears catalog. We would have to depend entirely on the charity of others for Christmas at our house this year. Again.

When the time came, there was always the waiting: would anyone remember us this year? Would we have any gifts, any celebration at all? Some years were better than others. Some years, no one came, and Mom just did the best she could.

After the holidays, I dreaded going back to school. There would always be the inevitable chore of "sharing with the class what you got for Christmas." "Pants that no one had worn before" would only bring laughter, so I would lie again. And there was that big girl in the front row who knew I was lying; one year she would tell the whole class, and I would run from the room.

I just wanted it to be over.

For many people, this will be the first holiday season without a loved one. For others, it will be the third, the fourth, or the tenth; the pain doesn't go away. Still others are alone this season, some in ways we can scarcely imagine: in prison, battling addiction, succumbing to illness, starving, abandoned, or living on the street. In all of this, Isaiah urges us to "Cry out!" (Is 40:6) He invites us to acknowledge our hurts, while offering us hope in the One who is to come.

Isaiah tells us it's ok to cry. It's ok to cry this Advent, this Christmas; it's ok to cry out in your desert. To cry when that special song is sung; to cry as you hang that extra angel on the tree. To cry for a childhood denied. To cry for words never spoken and for songs never sung. To cry for Christmas as it was last year, or the year before, or ten years ago; to cry for the Christmases that will never be again.

Our hearts hold the pain, struggles, wonderings, yearnings, and desires that lie deep within. Isaiah is urging us to cry out to God in the sadness, grief, joys, hopes, and yearnings of our hearts. Isaiah speaks of God's dwelling with us; he proclaims,

"Comfort, give comfort to my people" (Isaiah 40:1). He tells us that, if we hope in the Lord, we will "run and not grow weary, walk and not grow faint." (Isaiah 40:31) He assures us that our Heavenly Father is always at our side, and tells us "like a shepherd he feeds his flock and gathers the lambs in his arms." (Isaiah 40:11)

In saying all of this, Isaiah prepares us for the greatest message of all: "A young woman will bear a son and he shall be called Emmanuel – God is with us!"

Come, Lord Jesus!

**Reflection:**

**1.** Tell about an Advent season when you felt like "crying out in your desert." What made (or could have made) that time easier for you?

**2.** How have you been able to comfort someone else who was crying out?

**3.** How do you believe that God comforts those who are crying out to him?

## *The Fourth Chapter:*

# Trust His Grace

*"And since He bids me seek His face,*
*Believe His Word and trust His grace,*
*I'll cast on Him my every care,*
*And wait for thee, sweet hour of prayer"!*

*Sweet Hour of Prayer*
*William W. Walford, 1845*

*It has become a tradition, in the writing of our three books, that one reflection be written by the Editor (i.e., my son Jim) to give the Author (that would be me) the opportunity to take a little revenge for all of those classic and clever lines that ended up on the cutting-room floor during the editing process. So this reflection is by* ***James R. Welter II****, and it appears exactly as he wrote it – because I couldn't find one word that I would change! It's with considerable pride that I say: "Foiled again!"*

## *Kitties Know the Truth*

***Matthew 6:26***

*Look at the birds of the air: they neither sow nor reap nor gather into barns, and yet your heavenly Father feeds them. Are you not of more value than they?*

***Psalm 62:1, 8***

*For God alone my soul waits in silence;*
*from him comes my salvation. ...*

*Trust in him at all times, O people;*
*pour out your heart before him;*
*God is a refuge for us.*

**M**y wife Anna and I have two cats (or "kitties," as we affectionately call them, despite the fact that they have long since reached adulthood). I sometimes remark that they came with the house – because Anna let me know early on that having two cats was a prerequisite to owning a home with her! And when the proper time arrived, she exercised her option: one afternoon, not long after we had moved in, I was out in the backyard trimming tree branches when I saw Anna marching toward me like a woman on a mission. "I've found our kitties," she announced, "and I have to go get them!" I have never been much of a "pet person," as the pained expression on my face must have reminded her, but she was not to be dissuaded. "I told you before we bought the house that I wanted two cats, and you agreed," she said. "And I've finally found them online; now I have to go get them. Are you coming?"

The correct answer was not "no"... in fact, I'm probably lucky that she gave me enough time to put away my pruning saw and work gloves before we left!

We drove to the house of the woman Anna had found online who was selling kittens, picked out the two cutest ones (a male and female that sort of seemed to be a matched set), and took them home, stopping at the store along the way just long enough to quickly buy cat food, a pet bed, and a litter box. And from that day on, Kirby and Buttercup – as we named the two – became part of our family.

As I said, I am not generally a big fan of pets, so I was surprised at how quickly I grew to love our kittens (who grew up a lot faster than I expected). Kirby, especially, seemed born to be a "lap cat" and thrived on affection, often going out of his way to solicit petting or interaction, as if making a conscious effort to appeal to me. And as time went on, I began taking careful note of both his and Buttercup's behavior: how the two seemed to "forgive" my occasional (sometimes loud) grumbling about them getting underfoot, how one or the other would often come over and rub against me when I was feeling down, and how they almost always wanted to be near Anna and me, wherever we were in the house, no matter what we were doing... not for any particular reason, it appeared; they just seemed to enjoy being in our presence. And Kirby, in particular, would often pad into the kitchen when I was making something to eat (having heard the refrigerator door open from across the house!), and simply sit upright on the floor and look at me with big open eyes, as if waiting patiently. *I'm hungry, but I know you'll be with me shortly,* his behavior seemed to say. *I'll just wait here until you're ready to take care of me.*

And his apparent calm assurance that his "Daddy" would attend to his needs – his quiet, simple trust, and his willingness to wait in hope and expectation – one day brought the above passage from Matthew to my mind.

"Look at the birds of the air," Jesus says... and learn from their example. Learn of God's faithfulness: he cares for and provides for those who depend on him, knowing that they have no other recourse. Learn of God's generosity, for he gives what is needed, without merit or prerequisite. And learn that God never abandons those who are his own... not even the smallest of his creatures (Matthew 10:29).

Kirby's behavior reminded me that *our* attitude, looking at the example of the "birds of the air" (or, in this case, the "cat of the kitchen"!) should indeed be that of the Psalmist who counsels us to wait for God in silence, and trust him at all times to attend to our needs. Another translation of Psalm 62 puts the message even more directly and emphatically: we should depend on God alone, tell him all our troubles, put our hope in him, and wait patiently for him to save us – for he is our strong protector and our shelter... and we shall not be defeated!

This, to me, is the crux of what faith means – as exemplified in the behavior of one of God's small creatures. For if my little "kitty" evidently has such trust in *me*... why, then, should I doubt? *For if you know how to give good things to your "kitties,"* Jesus might say (paraphrasing Matthew 7:11)... *how much more will your Heavenly Father, in his infinite love and goodness, do for you?*

Perhaps this, then, expresses the essence of God's grace – that is, his unearned favor and goodwill, his undeserved kindness and mercy. And Jesus (like the Psalmist before him) tells us to *expect* this from God, and to rely on him always, without hesitation, just as his smallest creatures do. And just as one of them, in particular, relies on me.

So, when I find myself troubled, I often think of Kirby sitting patiently in my kitchen, waiting. And I try to imitate his simple faith and trust: *I'm in need, O Lord... but I know you won't abandon me; I'll wait patiently, until you're ready to take care of me... until you're ready to make your abundant grace known to me.*

Seeing their often blissfully serene behavior, their seemingly-unreserved trust, and their genuine love for the ones on whose "grace" they depend for nearly everything... I can't help but wonder if, indeed, we humans aren't needlessly anxious and worried about so many different things in life (as Jesus points out in Matthew 6:25-32)... while in contrast, as I sometimes half-jokingly put it, "kitties know the truth."

But maybe they do.

...now if only we can learn it as well!

### *What My Father Wants* *John 6:39-40*

*And this is the will of him who sent me, that I should lose nothing of all that he has given me, but raise it up on the last day. What my Father wants is this: that all those he has given me be saved.*

"Is she a drunk?" one old man asks another as they stare at a disheveled woman lying in the street. "Yep," the second man replies. "Been one all the years I've known her." "And before that?" the first man asks. "A whore up in Alaska, is what I've heard," comes the reply. "And before that?" the first man persists. "I don't know. Just a little kid, I guess."

I don't know how it will happen, but I believe that *everyone* will be saved!

If, as St. John says, that is what the Father wants, then I believe his grace will find a way. Grace sees the little kid – the innocent – in each of us, regardless of how sinfully defaced our image may have become. And I'm not convinced that it's too late even when we die! To believe that my chance to be saved is lost if I'm hit by a freight train seems to give that train power over God. Can that train really bring to an end to the saving power of God's grace? Can that freight train bring an end to the dream that God shares with his Son – "that all those he has given me be saved"?

I am aware that there are many scripture passages that can be quoted in opposition to my belief. But I believe many of those passages are taken out of context, because they have God act as we would act. So quoted, they often reveal a God who looks like us, acts like us, and thinks like we think! No – I will rest on the insight of St. John, who tells us that "God is love!" (1 John 4:8) Notice that he doesn't say that God *has* love, nor that God *shows* love... he says that God *is* love! In other words, it is the very nature of God to love; he can do no other. And St. Augustine, writing in the fifth century, reminds us that every passage in scripture (especially those that seem difficult to understand) must be interpreted in light of this knowledge. I would say it a little differently: if our interpretation of scripture creates for us an image of God that is different from the loving Father that Jesus revealed, then we must re-examine how we are interpreting scripture.

Taken in its entirety, scripture reveals a saving God who takes the initiative towards us: he's a loving father who runs to meet his prodigal son, a king who cancels a debt too large for his servant to repay, an employer who pays eleventh-hour workers the same as the first-hour crew, a banquet-giver who goes out to the highways and byways in search of "undeserving" guests, whom he then makes welcome. This is a God who does not forget even a tiny sparrow – much less us! (Luke 12:6-7)

Yet, like the characters we so often encounter in scripture, our tendency and need is to count and quantify, as we attempt to impose conditions on God's love and place limits on his grace. But God's grace is so free, so available, and such a great gift that it is virtually beyond our comprehension! So we are in good company with many characters in scripture when we try to quantify and limit that grace. Deep down, we often don't *like* other people to be the recipients of God's free gift! We want to get what we think we deserve – but we want others to get *what's coming to them!* In the parable of the laborers in the vineyard (Matthew 20:1-15), those who labor all day in the sun (that's us) expect to receive more than the late-comers – and when everyone is paid the same, we are indignant and accuse the master: "You treat *them* the same as *us!*" And the master replies: "I gave you what I promised – why are you envious of my generosity to others?"

Peter would understand; he loved to count and quantify Jesus' precise meaning. It is Peter who, in John's gospel, counts the number of fish caught when he is invited to cast his net on the other side of the boat (John 21:6-11). Quantifying and defining – or seeking some further, more precise assurance of our salvation – gives us the illusion of being in control of God's mercy and generosity. Jesus must have shaken his head: *poor Peter... he tries so hard, but he just doesn't get it!* There is no number! There are no limits. My grace, mercy, and forgiveness are always there for you.

At the Last Supper, Jesus shared a final meal with his friends, both to say goodbye and to show the way forward. But somehow, our liturgies often fail to capture the essence of that gathering. We fight about who is entitled to preside at the table; Jesus kneels at their feet. We argue about language; Jesus simply passes the bread and wine. We disagree about who belongs; Jesus feeds all who have come to him – even the one who will betray him.

The Last Supper exposes our shallow spirituality, as we seemingly work to distance ourselves from the meal's meaning: *God's amazing grace, given freely to all!* Bread broken, and wine poured out. New life, new hope, passed around in love. But we would rather dispute the details, as if God's giving depended on our defining!

"What my Father wants is... that all those he has given me be saved."

In ways we cannot (or perhaps just refuse to) imagine... I believe that, in the end... the Father will get what he wants!

**Reflection:**

**1.** What do you believe the scriptural phrase *"that all those he has given me be saved"* means? How did you come to your understanding of that phrase?

**2.** What image of God as a forgiving father speaks to you?

**3.** How does the Liturgy of the Eucharist meet (or sometimes fail to meet) your understanding of what Eucharist is, or should be?

### *First Born* *Micah 6:6a,7d, 8*

*With what shall I come before the LORD, and bow myself before God on high? Shall I give my firstborn for my transgression, the fruit of my body for the sin of my soul? He has told you, O man, what is good; and what does the LORD require of you but to do justice, and to love kindness, and to walk humbly with your God?*

"What we have here is... a failure to communicate!"

This is a classic line from the Paul Newman movie *Cool Hand Luke*... and it's also one of the most quoted lines in our house! My wife is an abstract thinker – she thinks in ideas, concepts, relationships, and visions. "When you look at the clouds, do you ever get homesick?" I sometimes ask her sarcastically (when she's not within earshot, of course!). I, on the other hand, deal in facts, plans, to-do lists, and all things concrete. As you might imagine, our "failures to communicate" are the stuff of legend!

What we have in the scripture passage above is also a "failure to communicate"!

The people are trying to make up for their sins by giving good things to God: "With what shall I come before the Lord?" Shall I come with burnt offerings? Will the Lord be pleased with thousands of rams or myriad streams of oil? "Shall I give my first-born for my transgression, the fruit of my body for the sin of my soul?"

But God seems discouraged: "My people, what have I done to you [to cause you think this way]? I brought you out of Egypt and released you from slavery. I sent you Moses and Arron and Miriam." (Micah 6:3-4) In other words, this was my free gift!

I didn't ask you to earn it or repay me! I don't need the things you offer; you know that I just want you to be faithful in your relationship with me. "You have been told what the Lord requires of you: [you need only] do what is right, love goodness, and walk humbly with your God."

The message I hear in this passage is that it's not that complicated! By the time Jesus arrived on the scene, the Ten Commandments had evolved into 613 Jewish laws – but Jesus summarized them all into two: Love God and love your neighbor!

In the gospels, Jesus frequently gets upset with the Pharisees because they seem preoccupied with defining, counting, and quantifying. They are so demanding that God do things *their* way, and fulfill the image they have created, that they miss the bigger picture. They miss the importance of being in a *relationship* with God.

For much of my life, I was preoccupied with sin and guilt. I was obsessed with defining, counting, measuring, and trying to make up for my failings; I was "sacrificing the fruit of my body for the sin of my soul"! But after much counseling and guidance, I'm finally okay with just releasing all that stuff to God's grace. The Catholic/Lutheran dialogues in the 1980s said it so well: "We are saved by grace to do good works." So I'm happy just to work in the vineyard – not because I *have* to in order to be saved, but because I *get* to... because I *am* saved! Nowadays, I'm content to keep it simple and live the words of that old Baptist hymn that my mother used to sing as she worked around the farmhouse: "*Just believe his word / And trust his grace.*"

There will be no "failure to communicate" if we listen carefully to the words of Micah! He tells us that we are not to become obsessed with our sins and shortcomings, but instead, that we are simply to "Do what is right, love kindness, and to walk humbly with our God." Amen!

**Reflection:**

**1.** How does one "walk humbly with God"?

**2.** When have you had to let go of what you knew or wanted, in order to walk humbly with God? How did doing so enhance your life?

**3.** Do you believe that God is involved in the decisions you make regarding the circumstances of your life? If so, how?

### *When the Hour Comes* *John 16:1-4*

*I have said all these things to you to keep you from falling away. They will put you out of the synagogues. Indeed, the hour is coming when whoever kills you will think he is offering service to God. And they will do these things because they have not known the Father, nor me. But I have said these things to you, that when their hour comes you may remember that I told you.*

"Wait until you have children of your own – *then* you'll understand!"

Has there ever been a parent who hasn't used those words? Most often, we use them out of frustration, when our child can't understand the feeling, emotion, experience, or idea we are trying to express. So we tell them to wait, so that when they have the experience, they will remember the lesson – and *will remember that we told them!*

Jesus has that same experience with his disciples. He realizes that much of what he has to tell them is beyond their experience, and beyond their ability to understand. They cannot conceive of a Messiah who will suffer, much less one who will die... and the idea of resurrection is far beyond their comprehension. So we find Jesus frequently using some version of the closing phrase in the scripture passage above: "And now I have told you before it takes place, so that when it does take place, you may believe." (John 14:29) "Do you not remember that when I was still with you I told you these things?" (2 Thessalonians 2:5).

There were things Jesus said that the disciples simply didn't want to hear, or even think about – and, to that extent, they were living in denial. They lived as if they didn't hear what

Jesus said. They lived as if what Jesus said would never happen. They lived in an illusion.

We, too, often live in an illusion. We are told again and again not to put our security in material things; Jesus tells us this, and the message is reinforced by spiritual leaders in every time and culture, in word and story. St. Matthew's gospel reminds us seven times that death or some life-changing event will occur, and we need to be ready because "we know not the day, nor the hour"!

Yet we still become engrossed in making a living, providing for our family, building our careers, and amassing possessions. And we are lulled by familiarity into believing that things will never change, and that no one can take away our "stuff"! It's a way of denying that life is uncertain. *Sure, it could happen,* we tell ourselves, *but not to me!* The arrow always hits the other guy!

Yet life has a way of reminding us of what Jesus said! As life shatters our illusions, one by one, we remember his words:

We tear down our barns and build new ones while amassing possessions to calm our insecurities.

*Remember that I told you...*

There's a downsizing at work and suddenly our income is gone.

*Remember that I told you...*

The economy turns and our retirement is suddenly "on hold."

*Remember that I told you...*

Our health fails and ordinary tasks become a daily challenge.

*Remember that I told you...*

A friend or relative dies, and we are left alone.

*Remember that I told you...*

We begin to measure our life in years remaining.

*Remember that I told you...*

And Spring bursts forth from the seeds that have fallen to the ground and died in Winter!

*Remember that I told you...*

**Reflection:**

**1.** In what ways have you lived in denial, but eventually come to see, believe, or understand?

**2.** What illusion in your life has been shattered? Does it reminds you of something that Jesus said?

**3.** Who in your life helps to shatter your illusions, so that you, too, may understand the words of Jesus more fully?

## *Tell the Others* *Acts 12:16-17*

*But Peter continued knocking, and when they opened, they saw him and were amazed. But motioning to them with his hand to be silent, he described to them how the Lord had brought him out of the prison. And he said, "Tell these things to James and the others."*

*(Nineteen ninety-five was a difficult year for me: on January 12, my mother died – and just eight weeks later, my sister Fran also died. Mom was 88 years old when she passed, and although she had raised seven children as a single parent under very difficult circumstances, she had only expressed one regret about her life: that she had never gotten to visit the Holy Land. On several previous occasions, I had promised Mom that I would visit the Holy Land for her. This is the story of a remarkable occurrence that happened on that trip.)*

I've been an accountant for most of my professional life. And, perhaps not surprisingly, I have the personality of an accountant: I love organization, predictability, exactness, order, and control. I am not given to believe in experiences that are not explainable, and I view with suspicion those who claim to see Jesus' image in the clouds, the Virgin Mary reflected in a window, or Mother Theresa's face in a biscuit!

It is from this perspective of natural skepticism that I relate one of the most profound and personal experiences of God at work in my life. I offer this story simply as my subjective experience, without editorial comment and without attempting to draw any conclusions. If I were telling the story today, I might use different words or phrases, or offer some new insight – after all, I'm not the same person now as I was back then. But I have chosen instead to simply share the thoughts I had at the time, as recorded in the daily journal I kept during my tour of the

Holy Land in 1995, and as told to my siblings in a letter I wrote shortly after my return home.

I leave it to you, the reader, to interpret matters as you will.

**The Letter:**

Dear Joe, Dot, Paul, Marty, and Hank:

I, like each of you, have been struggling to come to terms with Fran's untimely death. It is one thing to intellectually believe that Fran is in Heaven, and something else to be emotionally at peace with it. Helen had told me, from her own experience, that at some point I would know that it was okay that Fran died. It is okay with me now. I want to share with you how the peace I now feel came about. I understand that one person's miracle is another person's coincidence, so I won't attempt to draw conclusions for anyone. I'll just relate the incident, and my thoughts as I recorded them at the time, so each may draw whatever consolation may be found in the telling.

My trip to the Holy Land was, in part, keeping a promise to Mom that I would "go for her," since she lamented never being able to go there herself. The sense of awe one feels when walking where Jesus walked is beyond description and without comparison. The sense of being where all those stories we heard as children actually happened – those stories which became the bedrock of our faith and which carried us through so many hard times – formed a connectedness, a oneness, with this place that is hard to describe. I felt at home. I felt that I belonged there. It was *my* lake, *my* mountain, *my* desert, *my* city.

Our first Mass was on Pentecost Sunday. We celebrated on the roof of our hotel – with the Wall of old Jerusalem in the background. The contrast of old and new was striking. The old city, the root of our faith, where the Spirit first came, was in stark contrast to the gospel reading which challenged us to be open and to watch for *"The new thing I am about to do."*

My first night in the motel was spent in a basement room – a bit dark and musty, and not impressive. But that Sunday I was moved to a new room on the 4th floor, with a view of a bell tower on a hill in old Jerusalem.

***The rest is from my daily journal:***

"Bells awakened me at 5:00 a.m. My wake-up call had been left at the desk for 6:15. I peered out the window from my new room. The sun had not yet come up, but the orange light of a new day outlined the bell tower on the hill. "What a neat setting," I thought. "I'll read the scriptures assigned for today." The readings were from Luke's gospel, including chapter 11, verse 10: "For everyone who asks shall receive and he who seeks will find..." It was the line I had read at Fran's funeral.

As I read that line, the sun broke over the hill – so bright I couldn't look directly at it. I thought of Fran – and of Helen's remark that "Somehow, you will know it's all right that she died."

I drew the top curtain to reduce the brightness as I sank onto the couch with my head in my hands, wondering if this really was a sign. I prayed to be open to the Spirit this week, and to the "new things" I was to watch for.

A loud thud on the window caused me to look up – a bird had flown into the glass window, and now was hovering, outlined like a dove, its shadow formed by the bright sun, on my curtain. I felt the presence of the Spirit like no other time in my life, and an overwhelming assurance that Fran was at peace. The sense of God's presence was so real that I spoke out loud: “But, I miss her, Lord.” And the perceived response was just as real: “I know, but she is with me.”

The scripture reading from Acts – “Go and tell the others” – came immediately to mind. I feel compelled to share this with everyone in the family: Fran is with the Lord!

– ***End of Journal*** –

As I was flying back home, we were at 40,000 feet... the sky was a perfect blue as far above the plane and as far out as I could see, and below was the blue of the Mediterranean Sea. In a strange yet comforting way, I felt a part of it all. I felt at one with this universe of perfect color. “You would have enjoyed the trip, Mom,” I murmured aloud.

“I did,” she said.

**Reflection:**

**1.** What concrete experience of God’s presence in your life have you wanted to share with others? When and how have you done so?

**2.** If someone relates their experience of God’s presence in a way you don’t understand or believe, how do you react to it? Why? Is it possible that God speaks to different people in different ways? Why or why not?

**3.** How do you think we can become more aware of God’s presence in our daily life?

***Who Do You Say That I Am?***

***Matthew 16:13-16***

*Now when Jesus came into the district of Caesarea Philippi, he asked his disciples, "Who do people say that the Son of Man is?" And they said, "Some say John the Baptist, others say Elijah, and others Jeremiah or one of the prophets." He said to them, "But who do you say that I am?" Simon Peter replied, "You are the Christ, the Son of the living God."*

**I**n this scripture passage, Jesus asks his disciples "...who do you say that I am?" And Peter quickly responds, *"You are the Christ, the Son of the living God."* Impressed, Jesus calls Peter *"blessed"* and says *"...upon this rock I will build my Church."*

But when Jesus is arrested, Peter undergoes a dramatic reversal. Identified as a follower of Jesus, he fervently denies it and says, *"I am not [one of his disciples]!"* (John 18:25).

Too often, I am like Peter. I know who *Jesus* is – but I'm not ready to accept *my* identity as part of the Body of Christ. Like Peter, I believe that accepting that identity will require too much of me.

So, like Peter, I deny who Christ calls me to be. Perhaps I resist a call to change how I interact with others, or to welcome more intimate relationships. Or maybe I resist a call to be more other-centered – to love my neighbor, or to welcome *everyone* as my neighbor.

Our decisions – our responses to Jesus' call – help to define who we are. They did so for Peter. While he knew who Jesus was, the more important – and more difficult – question was "Who is *Peter*?" In the courtyard after Jesus' arrest, Peter denied who Jesus called him to be... three times.

But God loved Peter too much to accept his denials as the last word! Even as Jesus was crucified (and Peter did nothing), God had plans for Peter. The risen Christ called to the disciples as they were fishing; he called them to a cookout on the beach. And Christ asked Peter three times, "Do you love me?" And three times, Peter affirmed who he was – and who he would become.

As with Peter, Christ loves us too much to accept yesterday's denials as the last word! Today, he again calls us to love him – to feed his lambs, to tend his lambs, to feed his sheep.

Who will deliver Christ's call to me today?

And will I say "yes" to who Christ calls me to become?

***William Bradbury***

*(Bill Bradbury was one of the first people to say "yes" to my invitation to write for the St. Monica e-mail reflection ministry, and he has been sharing his scripture insights for more than twelve years. In addition, he has served as that ministry's administrator for many years. It has been under Bill's tutelage that an unexpected dimension of the ministry has flourished – that of interaction with our readers and of supporting many during difficult times. It is my privilege and blessing to call Bill my friend. – Jim Welter)*

**Reflection:**

**1.** Tell about a person in your life who delivered Christ's call to you. How did that occur?

**2.** Did you deny who Christ called you to be at some time or in some circumstances in your life? How?

**3.** When did you say "yes" to who Christ called you to be? How did that change your life?

### *We Miss the Signs* **Mark 8:11-19**

*The Pharisees came and began to argue with him, seeking from him a sign from heaven to test him. And he sighed deeply in his spirit and said, "Why does this generation seek a sign? Truly, I say to you, no sign will be given to this generation." And he left them, got into the boat again, and went to the other side.*

The Hebrews of Jesus' time watched in great anticipation for some sign that the Messiah had come. They expected the Messiah to come as a great ruler, with the power to take back their land and restore them to the glory days of King David. And Jesus "sighed deeply in his spirit" when the Pharisees again asked him for a sign.

Jesus was frustrated because he had already provided many signs: he quoted their own scriptures, he multiplied the loaves, he walked on water, and he even raised the dead. But the people didn't get it. They had preconceived ideas of what the Messiah would look like and how he would act – and Jesus didn't fit those preconceptions. They missed the signs!

Whether I am lonely, sad, frustrated, restless, tired, angry, cold, hungry, depressed, destitute, unemployed, or homeless, I too want a sign that God is with me. Asking for a sign from God is not a bad thing; God has promised us signs. But a genuine request for a sign flows from an open heart: it stems from an honest seeking of God's will, and a willingness to accept God's answer, even if it is not the one we wanted. We often come to prayer with our answers defined and our parameters set – and so, we often miss the signs!

The Messiah has come! Jesus is in our midst! He lives in a thousand homeless people in this very city – but we miss the sign.

*"I am alone in the streets of this city and no one sees me. No one is looking for me. No one knows who I am. No one knows who I was or where I came from."*

We miss the sign.

*"I huddle in the doorways at night. I sleep under the bridge on rainy days. I sleep on the beach and in the park. I am alone."*

We miss the sign.

*"I pick up your cigarette butts tossed on the street and I go through your trash thrown out. I am alone."*

We miss the sign.

*"I miss my home. I miss my parents and my brothers and sister, my aunts and uncles. God knows, I miss my children. I am alone."*

We miss the sign.

Come down from that cross – then I will believe! Do it *my* way, and my faith will be strong. Give me the miracle I've been praying for; then I will be convinced. Multiply the loaves again and feed this homeless person.

No wonder Jesus sighs.

We miss the sign.

*(The four quotes above are excerpted from* No One Sees Me, *a book by David Sleppy that is a pictorial reflection on homelessness in America. They are used with permission.)*

**Reflection:**

**1.** What signs that God is with you do you tend to look for in your troubled times? Have you often seen them?

**2.** Looking at your life, what signs of "God with us" might you have missed in a time of loss or grief? Who or what has helped you to see "the signs" in those times?

**Hold On** ***John 11:20-27***

*When Martha heard that Jesus was coming, she went to meet him; but Mary sat at home. Martha said to Jesus, "Lord, if you had been here, my brother would not have died. (But) even now I know that whatever you ask of God, God will give you." Jesus said to her, "Your brother will rise." Martha said to him, "I know he will rise, in the resurrection on the last day." Jesus told her, "I am the resurrection and the life; whoever believes in me, even if he dies, will live, and everyone who lives and believes in me will never die. Do you believe this?" She said to him, "Yes, Lord. I have come to believe that you are the Messiah, the Son of God..."*

**M**y mother raised seven children alone on a broken-down old farm, and was almost eighty-eight years old when she died in 1995. We had talked of death many times; she couldn't understand why she had lived so long. "Even the people I knew at the senior citizens center have all died," she remarked one evening. Mom was ready to go.

As Mom's funeral began on that January morning, all seven of us walked behind her casket into our country church in Knox, Indiana. All seven of us had been baptized in that church. All seven of us had received our first communion there, and had been raised in the Catholic faith in that church. As we entered, we sang one of Mom's favorite old Baptist hymns: "*Sweet hour of prayer / Sweet hour of prayer / That takes me from / This world of care.*"

We laid Mom to rest in a little cemetery near our old farm. Her grave stands next to that of our infant sister, who had died more than fifty years before.

The death of a parent has its own special grief. Mom's death was difficult, but it seemed right; we were all adults, and it was the next normal step in life.

But eight weeks later, we were back in that same church. This time we walked in behind the casket of my sister Fran. We sang that same hymn – but this time it didn't seem right. This time every fiber of my being screamed, "Why, Lord?! Why my sister? Why Frannie? Why now, so soon after Mom?"

An out-of-sequence death has its own particular pain. In this gospel passage, Martha screams for all of us: "If you had been here, Lord, my brother would not have died!" And Jesus replies, "Your brother will rise." "I know, Lord, on the last day!" But Jesus looks into our eyes: "*I* am the resurrection and the life." I'm not talking about some nebulous future time! Today, your sister, your brother, your parent, your spouse, your child – lives! "Do you believe this?"

Martha answers for all of us: I've never seen a life beyond this one; never known anyone to rise from the dead. This isn't part of my experience. And it hurts so much. But she says, "I have come to believe you are the Messiah." I believe in you!

When it feels like our very lives have been ripped from us – when our pain is beyond the telling – like Martha, sometimes all we can do is hold on and say: "I believe in you, O Lord. I believe in you!"

**Reflection:**

**1.** What event in your life has caused you to ask God "why?" How did you resolve your questioning?

**2.** What is your understanding of "life everlasting"?

**3.** What sustains you in being able to say "Yes, Lord, I believe"? Can you?

### *Grandma Doesn't Live Here*

***Ecclesiastes 3:1-6***

*For everything there is a season, and a time for every matter under heaven: a time to be born... and a time to die; a time to plant... and a time to uproot; a time to weep... and a time to laugh; a time to mourn... and a time to dance; a time to keep ... and a time to let go.*

"If there is a Hell," my wife often remarks when the subject comes up, "I believe there are at least three people there: Judas, Hitler – and the doctor who put the feeding tube in my mother!"

My mother-in-law Carolyn (who insisted that all her sons-in-law call her "Mom") was an independent, strong-willed person, like many of German heritage who were raised in the rural setting of Southern Indiana. "I don't want anyone to ever have to take care of me," she would say with increased frequency as the years went by. "And, if it ever comes to being hooked up to those machines to stay alive, I don't want it!" "We know that, Mom; we all know that." She had seven children, but sometimes even we in-laws would chime in: "Even the mailman knows that, Mom! It won't happen."

My mother-in-law suffered a stroke from which she seemed, at first, to recover. In the few weeks that followed, she elicited the promise one final time: no machines. Her second stroke left her partially paralyzed, and in a vegetative state in which she was unable to communicate or recognize anyone.

When the question of a feeding tube first came up, the answer was obvious to everyone. "But, Mr. Fritz," the doctor counseled my father-in-law (with no other family members present), "I've seen people in your wife's condition get well. What do you have to lose? If she doesn't respond in a few weeks, we'll take it out."

Mom didn't respond. And when the family finally asked that the tube be removed, they were informed by that same doctor: "Oh, we can't do that – it's against the law!"

Mom was to remain in that vegetative state for two-and-a-half years. My father-in-law visited her in the nursing home twice a day, every day, the entire time she was there. She was never able to acknowledge his presence or that of any other family member. In the end, she died alone.

Scientific advances now allow us to live through illnesses or injuries which, only a few years ago, would have killed us. Yet this same technology also tells us the "big lie": that science can solve all our problems, and can save us from everything that's bad. Technology beckons us to its institutions (i.e., hospitals, nursing homes) to die – and in America, eighty percent of us come. We come because of our own fears. We come because of the "big lie" in our society, in which commercials whisper that you can stay young forever if you use the right products or take the right medicines! Advertisers would apparently have us believe that aging isn't normal – and that death is ultimately avoidable! Society whispers: *your value is in your possessions... you are what you have, and nobody can take it from you!* And we believe the lie, and put our security in material things. We live in the false belief that death will never come. And the pumping of a respirator, the drip of an IV, tells us it is so!

In expressing the Christian obligation to respect life in all its forms, the late Cardinal Joseph Bernardin coined a beautiful phrase: the "seamless garment." He stated that a Christian must "weave a seamless garment" – which means that we must be consistent in our opposition to any act which does violence to the sacredness of life, whether it is abortion, suicide, the death penalty, euthanasia, or war.

As a Christian, I believe that life is sacred. I believe that life has a value that is inherent and beyond our right or prerogative to control. But I also believe that the seamless garment – that respect for life – must also somehow include the permission to die. I believe that to disrupt the natural flow of life – to put a seam in its fabric by not letting it end naturally – is also to do it violence.

One day, while visiting the nursing home, one of the small children of the family was observing my mother-in-law (her "Grandma"). She noticed how the body was frozen in an unnatural position, and how the formerly heavy and healthy person had now become a mere skeleton of her former self.

"That doesn't look like Grandma," she remarked to no one in particular. "It isn't," her big sister replied. "Grandma doesn't live here anymore!"

**Reflection:**

**1.** As a Christian, to what extremes do you believe one must or should go to in order to preserve a human life? Is there a point at which a person's existence *stops* being anything which can meaningfully be called a "human life"? If so, what do you believe should be done, or not done, for the person at that point?

**2.** Psychologists often refer to us as a "death-denying society." What societal behaviors do you think support this statement?

**3.** Denial of anything usually reveals an underlying fear. What fears cause us to deny or be uncomfortable with death? How might these fears be overcome? Or can they be?

**4.** What does our fear of or discomfort with death say about us as Christians? How do you think a Christian should view, and deal with, death?

### ***Blessed Are You Poor*** ***Luke 6:20-21***

*And raising his eyes toward his disciples he said: "Blessed are you who are poor, for the kingdom of God is yours. Blessed are you who are now hungry, for you will be satisfied."*

Anyone who knows me knows that I don't eat chicken. Our boys always found that humorous: they were convinced it was because, as a child, I once got pecked on the head by a rooster! (I should never have told them that story!) But I'm sure it was actually due to my experiences as a child growing up on the family farm: when we had nothing else to eat, our last resort was to kill a chicken.

I remember a time when we were down to our last chicken. We had only one chicken with which to feed nine people for three days. When I recently shared that story with a friend, his response was, "Oh, I like chicken salad!" He couldn't conceive of abject poverty: there was no salad, no bread, no salt, no milk – just one chicken. For nine people. For three days.

"Blessed are you who are poor," says Jesus in Luke's gospel. As a poor, hungry child, I sure didn't feel very blessed! And one day, a man came into my office at St Monica parish who didn't feel blessed, either: he and his family had been living in a car for several days. Would any of us volunteer for these kinds of "blessings"? So what is Jesus talking about here? How can one possibly find happiness in poverty, hunger, suffering, and sorrow?

Few of us would seek poverty, nor would a loving God give it to us as some kind of test, or as a means of teaching us a lesson. The uncomfortable truth is that people are not poor because God neglects them – but because *we* do. Poverty exists because we do not fully respond to the needs of one another. Yet the poor are forced to depend on God, because they often have nowhere else to turn. They know they are not in control of their lives; they know that they cannot do it by themselves. They live in faith, and in their emptiness, they turn to God. And they come to know what we so often forget: that everything is a gift, that everything we have is through God's grace. Only when our hands are empty are we open to receive; only when we are hungry can we be filled.

As we sat down to eat our last chicken, my father began to pray: "Bless us, O Lord, and these thy gifts..." My sister and I started to cry. "Why should we pray," we asked, "when all we have to eat is one puny chicken?" I was only five years old, but I remember the look of surprise on my father's face; it would never have occurred to him to do anything else. "We give thanks," he answered, "for whatever we are given."

Blessed are you who are poor, for the kingdom of God is yours.

**Reflection:**

**1.** Tell about a time that it was difficult for you to thank God for what you had been given. What did you do or say?

**2.** How do you keep greatfulness alive in your life?

**3.** What might you do to connect with those who live in poverty?

### *The Fiery Furnace* **Matthew 13:41-43**

*The Son of Man will send his angels, and they will gather out of his kingdom all causes of sin and all law-breakers, and throw them into the fiery furnace. In that place there will be weeping and gnashing of teeth. Then the righteous will shine like the sun in the kingdom of their Father.*

**A** scripture passage like this one raises a lot of questions. The vision of sinners being thrown into a fiery furnace presents us with a stern, judgmental image of God that seems inconsistent with the loving Father that Jesus revealed. Fortunately, we do not have to analyze the text or examine the circumstances that influenced the writer for the passage to have meaning to us. All we have to do is ask: how does this scripture passage apply to *me?*

I hear this passage challenging me to gather up and cast away those parts of my life that are not "of God" – that is, those things that prevent me from becoming my highest and best self. So I must ask myself: what "causes of sin" in my life do I need to throw into the "fiery furnace"?

Certainly any grudges or resentments that I bear toward others should be on my "burn list"! Negative thoughts that would deny God's goodness by leading me to believe I have no special gifts or talents also need to be cast into the flames. A belief that good cannot come out of my current situation (whatever it may be) needs to go, too. I'll have to take a long look at my goals, my relationships, and my attitudes – to determine how big that fire needs to be!

One of the most painful elements in my life that I had to "cast away" was my tendency to define myself by the job I held.

To move from saying "I am an accountant" to saying "I am a person who does accounting" took years of struggle and required a lot of painful growth. But that old, limiting self-image has been burning in the "fiery furnace" for quite a while now – and from that furnace has emerged an author, a pastoral minister, a public speaker, and a much more well-rounded (and, I hope, a kinder and gentler) human being!

The highlight of this transformation came one Sunday morning when I was invited to preach the gospel at St. Thomas Aquinas, which was the church of my childhood. The pulpit from which I spoke was just a few steps from the pew in which, as a teenager, I had sat and trembled with fear before the God of the "fiery furnace"! But that fear has long since been cast away, and I spoke instead of the God whom I now know: the caring Creator who comes down from heaven and walks in the garden with us. The Good Shepherd who brings his lost sheep home. The loving Father who sacrificed his only Son for me.

What must you "cast into the fiery furnace," so you can see what God wants you to see – and be who he wants you to become?

**Reflection:**

**1.** What is on your "burn list"? What are you willing to cast into the "fiery furnace" today?

**2.** When the old "you" has been burned away, what new thing in you do you think might emerge? What do you think God wants *you* to see and know about yourself?

**3.** Can you reconcile a God of justice with a God of mercy? If so, how?

**_Back Home Again_** **_Luke 2:46-49_**

*After three days they found him in the temple, sitting in the midst of the teachers, listening to them and asking them questions, and all who heard him were astounded at his understanding and his answers. When his parents saw him, they were astonished, and his mother said to him, "Son, why have you done this to us? Your father and I have been looking for you with great anxiety." And he said to them, "Why were you looking for me? Did you not know that I must be in my Father's house?"*

I remember being separated from my mother when I was eight or nine years old. She anxiously searched the store where we were shopping, and when she finally found me, I couldn't believe she was upset: "I was only looking at the toys, Mom!"

In this gospel story, Jesus has been lost for several days. He is about twelve years old, and his parents, anxious and worried, have been searching madly for him. When they finally find him, Jesus can't believe they are upset: "Didn't you know that I must be in my Father's house?"

In writing his gospel, Luke uses the theme of a journey. Less than halfway through his story, Luke tells us that Jesus "set his face toward Jerusalem," (Luke 9:51) and the rest of Luke's gospel is the story of that journey. It isn't surprising, then, that at the end of his life, in the final days before his death on the cross, we find Jesus back in Jerusalem – back in his Father's house. The circle is complete; the journey ends where it began.

The circle we see in Luke's gospel calls to mind the circle of our own life. Genesis tells us that "God took the soil of the ground and blew into it the breath of life." The life in us is the breath of God – and when God breathes in again, we die. God draws us back to himself, back to the source of life from which we came, and our body returns to the soil. The circle is complete; the journey ends where it began.

Our loved ones who have died must surely be as mystified by our sorrow as Jesus was when his parents found him in the temple. "Why are you looking for me?" they might ask. Do you not know that the circle is complete, and the journey ends where it began? Do you not know that God has breathed in again, and I am home?

Do you not know that I must be in my Father's house?

**Reflection:**

**1.** Have your ideas or feelings about death changed over the years? How? Why?

**2.** Have you had the experience in your life of being on a journey? How did you feel when the journey was completed?

**3.** What images of the circle of life have meaning for you?

**_Go to Galilee_** **_Matthew 28:8-10_**

*So they departed quickly from the tomb with fear and great joy, and ran to tell his disciples. And behold, Jesus met them and said, "Greetings!" And they came up and took hold of his feet and worshiped him. Then Jesus said to them, "Do not be afraid; go and tell my friends to go to Galilee, and there they will see me."*

**E**aster has come – but you're still unemployed! Easter has come – but your loved one is still sick or dying! Easter has come – and that special relationship still isn't working! Easter has come – and those old habits and addictions still have power! Easter has come – but your cancer is still growing!

The Eastern Orthodox Christians refer to the first Monday after Easter as "Bright Monday." It is called "bright" because, through Christ's rising, a light now shines in the darkness of our problems, and even in death itself. The Easter Season's scripture readings speak of changes – not in Jesus, but in those around him. Just as a bright light transforms objects previously shadowed in darkness, so does the Resurrection of Jesus have the power to transform our lives.

Then Jesus said to them, "Do not be afraid. Go and tell my friends to go to Galilee, and there they will see me."

Galilee was where it all began, where they were first called to follow him. In times of trial or stress, we too often return to our roots to gather strength. We return to the place where *we* were first called. We go to our "Galilee" to gain a renewed sense of who we are, and what we believe.

We don't go to Galilee to relive the past. We can't go back and undo the wrongs, correct the mistakes, or make our problems go away. We go to Galilee to come to *terms* with our past – to struggle with all that has changed in our lives, and to adjust to our new reality. We go to Galilee to figure out how we will live in the "new normal" of our everyday existence.

We won't get our old life back in Galilee. We won't get our health back. We won't get our friends or loved ones back. We don't go to Galilee to change our beginnings. We go to Galilee to start where we are now – and change our endings!

**Reflection:**

**1.** What things in your past do you need to come to terms with in order to change the ending? How can you begin to do this today?

**2.** What does it mean to you to "start where we are now"?

**3.** What "new normal" have you experienced because of changes you have made in your life? How has that affected you?

***Emmaus*** ***Luke 24:13-16***

*Now that very day two of them were going to a village seven miles from Jerusalem called Emmaus, and they were conversing about all the things that had occurred. And it happened that while they were conversing and debating, Jesus himself drew near and walked with them, they saw him, but didn't recognize him.*

It isn't surprising to find that one of the last stories in St. Luke's gospel is about a journey: that's Luke's format throughout his entire gospel and in the book of Acts.

It is the first Easter Sunday, and two disciples are on the road to Emmaus, which is "about seven miles from Jerusalem." Jesus is dead. He apparently wasn't who – or what – they thought he was. Their hopes are dashed, so they're hanging it up. Calling it quits. Going back home.

Suddenly, Jesus is walking with them on the road. Scripture says, "They saw him, but didn't recognize him." Didn't recognize him?! The women had been told by angels that Jesus was alive; the Easter message had been proclaimed. But they didn't recognize him! He recited scripture until their "hearts were burning," but they didn't recognize him! He "interpreted every passage of scripture that pertained to him" – he gave them all the facts – and they *still* didn't recognize him!

Then something happens that makes all the difference. Night is coming, and it looks like Jesus will be moving on. They could have said good-bye, like we do when we meet an interesting person on a plane: "It was nice meeting you; hope you have a nice trip..." And it's over. Our life doesn't change.

But instead, they say: "Stay with us." (A richer translation puts it: "Abide with us.") Break bread, share a meal, enter into a relationship with us... be part of our lives.

When they extend that invitation, Jesus takes over. There is a reversal of roles, and Jesus breaks the bread. The stranger becomes a friend. The invited guest becomes the host. And in the sharing of a meal, in that intimate relationship – they recognize him!

Luke seems to be saying that, to know Jesus, we must invite him in. And, if we do that – he will take over our lives! And we will recognize him!

It is significant that Luke only names one of the disciples on that road: it is his way of inviting us into the story. *We* are the other disciple! And Luke invites us to walk the journey, and to encounter Jesus and recognize him.

Each of us is in a different place on that journey. Some have not yet met Jesus. Others have met Jesus, but do not recognize him in a personal way in their lives. Still others recognize Jesus, and are challenged to live out of that experience.

Do we recognize Jesus on our journey? To recognize him, we must invite him in. And if we invite him in... he will take over our lives!

How will you recognize Jesus today?

**Reflection:**

**1.** How do you invite Jesus into your daily life?

**2.** What does it mean to say that, if you invite Jesus in, he will take over your life?

**3.** In what ways can we acknowledge that we recognize Jesus?

***The Only Thing That Matters***

***1 Corinthians 13:1-8,13***

*If I speak in human tongues and angelic as well, but have not love, I am a noisy gong or a clanging cymbal. And if I have the gift of prophecy, and understand all mysteries and all knowledge, and if I have faith enough to move mountains, but have not love, I am nothing. If I give everything I have to the poor and surrender my body to be burned, but have not love, I gain nothing.*

*Love is patient. Love is kind. Love does not envy or boast; it is not proud or rude. Love is not self-seeking, it is not easily angered, and it keeps no record of injuries. Love does not delight in evil but rejoices with the truth. Love bears all things, believes all things, hopes all things, endures all things. Love never fails. As for prophecies, they will pass away; as for tongues, they will cease; as for knowledge, it too will pass away.*

*And now these three remain: faith, hope and love. But the greatest of these is love.*

*(Not only did I have the privilege of going to college at the same time as my two sons, but they both asked me to read from scripture at their wedding – and both happened to choose the same passage from St. Paul's letter to the church at Corinth. While my message was basically the same for each occasion, the settings were as unique and different as our two sons! Mark and Lori stood before the stained-glass window that I designed for the Emmaus Center at St. Monica Parish, depicting Jesus on the road to Emmaus. Four years later, Jim and Anna stood on a beach in Aruba before the setting sun and blue waters of the Caribbean Sea. Both invitations to proclaim the word on these special occasions were priceless gifts to me. This is the text of my message.)*

**M**ark and Lori. Jim and Anna. The Lord would have you know this today... in the end, there are only three things that matter: faith, hope, and love – and the greatest of these is love.

The passage we just heard contains some of the most beautiful lines in scripture. We often hear them read at weddings, and we see them captured in cross-stitched pillows or etched on wall plaques. They're appropriate for those uses – but we can be sure that's *not* what St. Paul had in mind!

To appreciate the power of these words, we need to hear them in context: St. Paul was writing to a community in turmoil. The Christians in Corinth were maneuvering for leadership positions, making judgments about who was worthy to come to the table, and arguing about who had the most talent. So Paul writes a letter and tells them that those things don't matter. He reminds them that the only thing that matters is that we love each other. And then he tells them what love is: love is patient and kind, love believes all things, hopes all things, endures all things. And those words become a mirror for us to hold up in our marriage relationship: *am I patient? Am I kind? Do I believe? Am I committed?*

Jim and Anna; Mark and Lori, everyone here wishes for you those things that really matter!

We wish you *faith* – may you always believe in the goodness you find in each other today.

We wish you *hope* – not hope as wishful thinking, but hope as an expectation that good will come from all of the experiences in your life together.

We wish you *love* – for your love will define who you are as a person, and as a couple.

Because everything in your life together will flow from that love, it *is* – as St. Paul says – the greatest gift.

And, in the end... it's the only thing... that matters!

**Reflection:**

**1.** What would it look like to you to truly live life out of love?

**2.** What would you have to change in yourself to be able to live out of only those things that really matter?

**3.** In what circumstances are you inclined *not* to live out of love? Why? What can you do to change that?

### *Castles in the Sand* *Matthew 18:2-3*

*He called a child over, placed it in their midst, and said, "Amen, I say to you, unless you turn and become like children, you will not enter the kingdom of heaven."*

It's summer, a lazy Sunday afternoon. The sunlight glistens on the water as the waves gently wash to shore. The beach stretches as far as the eye can see. A child plays in the sand: he builds a castle, and then another. As the sun moves slowly across the sky, a moat emerges and water is brought from the sea in a hundred trips.

Now the sun is low, and the waves increase. "Time to go!" calls a voice from the shore.

The child laughs, watching as everything he has built is washed away. He knows he can't take his castles with him. The joy is in the building. The music is in the song that is sung. The goal is the journey. In the end, all is washed back to the sea.

It is as it should be.

The day has ended. The child laughs with glee, takes his father's hand, and goes home.

"Unless you become as a little child," Jesus says, "you cannot enter the kingdom."

Throughout our lives, we build our castles, toil in the sun, make a hundred trips to the sea.

"Time to go!" calls a voice from the shore.

The day has ended.

May we, too, know we can't take our castles with us. The joy is in the building. The music is in the song that is sung. The goal is the journey. In the end, all is washed back to the sea.

It is as it should be.

When we hear that voice, may we laugh with glee, take our Father's hand... and go home.

### *Snow Is Falling Somewhere* *1 John 4:8*

*"Whoever is without love does not know God, for God is love."*

I don't know the name of the song, but I think of it every time the snow falls. The singer compares the love of Jesus to the falling snow: the snow falls on everything, the just and the unjust, the rich and the poor; it covers our failures, our imperfections, and our sinfulness. And "snow is falling somewhere, like the love of Jesus."

It's the only line I remember. It's the only line I need.

It is snowing in Indiana, our first of the season, as I write this. I'm enjoying it. I'm delaying going to Mass so I don't have to go out in it, and ignoring the fact that, before the end of the day, I'll be shoveling it from our steps. I am choosing instead to pray with it; to listen to its silence and marvel at its beauty. To let it return me to my childhood on the farm.

Our children are now adults; I'm not going to get away with making snow cream today. Maybe I can manage chili for lunch, though. We always had chili on the cold, snowy days. Maybe I can huddle with my sister Fran again, share our hopes for the future, and make pictures in the frost on the window.

Fran has been gone more than fifteen years now. But I feel her presence today.

"Snow is falling somewhere..."

I love you, Frannie.

## *Come Before Winter*

The year is 67 A.D., and the apostle Paul is nearing the end of his life. He languishes in a jail cell in Rome, awaiting trial and possible execution. Even if he is spared, his frail and tired body won't last much longer. He has only two friends who have not deserted him: there is Luke, the "beloved physician" who was "with Paul until the end," and Timothy, whom he calls "my own son in the faith" (1Timothy 1:2). In that cold and dreary cell, Paul remembers an old cloak he had left in Troas. He writes to Timothy, and asks him to visit – and, on his way, to pick up his cloak and some books he had also left there (2 Timothy 4:13). Near the end of the letter, he adds: "Come before Winter" (2 Timothy 4:21).

Paul didn't just ask Timothy to come as soon as he could – he made a point of adding "before Winter." In Paul's time, navigation in the Mediterranean stopped in wintertime; no boats would be running and it would be impossible to travel. In other words, if Timothy didn't come before Winter, it would be too late.

It is said that "opportunity knocks but once." Not true; opportunity knocks many times – but it *is* true that there will come a *last* time opportunity will knock! When Paul wrote asking Timothy to visit, it was before Winter... or never. Even in that mundane, practical request for his cloak, St. Paul is teaching us: don't wait too long, don't put things off and miss your chance. Come before Winter.

One sure thing about the season of Autumn is that Winter will soon follow. Although we don't know exactly when it will arrive, we know that it will come. On the farm, there were certain jobs to do before Winter, and there was a sense of urgency to get them done, because no one knew exactly when Winter would come. The first snowfall was often a surprise.

So it is with our lives: Spring and Summer pass, and it's Autumn before we know it. Time moves quickly, and we are unaware of the passing years. It seems as if it were yesterday that I was young, newly married, and embarking on my life with my chosen one... yet, in a way, it also seems like it was long ago, and I wonder where the years have gone. I know that I lived them all; I have recollections of how it was back then, and of all my hopes and dreams... but here it is, the Autumn of my life, and it still catches me by surprise. How did I get here so fast? Where did the time go? Where did my little boys go? Where did my youth go? And who is that old man who stares back at me each time I look in the mirror?

The stanza of an old song we used to sing has new meaning now: *"Those were the days, my friend / We thought they'd never end / We'd sing and dance / Forever and a day..."* How could we have known the truth of the words we sang with so much laughter?

And now I find that I enter into this new season of my life unprepared for its limitations and losses. But at least I know that Autumn has come... and I know that Winter will surely follow. And so I make different choices, and live life with a greater sense of urgency.

If you're not in *your* Autumn yet, let me forewarn you: it will be here sooner than you think. So, whatever you'd like to accomplish with your life – do it soon!

*Come before Winter...*

Don't put things off for too long; life goes by quickly.

*Come before Winter...*

Do what you can *today;* you have no guarantee that you will live to see all the seasons of your life.

*Come before Winter...*

My father died at age 90 when I was a young adult, but I never said to him: "I love you."

*Come before Winter...*

Some of my relatives have not spoken to each other in years; even *they* don't know what the issues are, or were, any longer.

*Come before Winter...*

Most fathers plan to be a friend to their children... but fathers need to work. There is business and golf, dinner meetings, and the need to sleep late on the weekends. But children don't wait – they grow up.

*Come before Winter...*

We always think there will be more time. If you have unresolved issues with a loved one, address them now.

*Come before Winter...*

Is there an un-reconciled relationship in your life? Let go of the need to be right, and forgive someone today.

*Come before Winter...*

My fondest hope and most persistent prayer is that any unresolved issues with my children will be resolved. ("Ask any questions you have about your childhood while I'm still here to answer," I tell them.)

*Come before Winter...*

Try to say all the things you want your loved ones to remember, while you can.

*Come before Winter...*

...and bring my cloak, and my books. Bring those things that give me comfort. Bring your friendship, your support, and your love. And please, do your best to...

*Come before Winter...*

# The End of Autumn

As I stand on the threshold of a new beginning,
I remember all those who have gone before me.
They give me strength.

I am mindful of those who follow me.
I offer them hope.

I feel now a curious blend of grief and gladness, over the endings that this season brings. Still, I praise you for the journey.

I praise you for the truth of love – and the value of friendships.

I praise you for the miracle of life – and the power of growth.

I praise you for the bends in the road that have strengthened me – and the faith that has carried me through the tough times.

Help me to faithfully move into my future and as I continue my journey.

Father, grant that I treasure all that is gift and blessing – and hold all life in open hands.

Grant, too, that I receive the truth of your presence – and that I am open to the gift of your grace.

For all that has been, Father – I say thank you.

For all that is to come – I say yes!

# INDEX
## By Reflection Title

# INDEX
By Bible Chapter & Verse

## OLD TESTAMENT

## NEW TESTAMENT

### Matthew



### Mark



### Luke

**Luke *(Continued)***



**John**



**Acts**



**Romans**



**1 Corinthians**



**Galatians**



**2 Thessalonians**



**1 John**

You may order additional copies of

# *Some Call it Autumn*

on our website, **www.AscendingView.com**

OR

Send check or Money Order for $14.95 per copy
plus $3.00 shipping and handling
(Indiana residents add 7% sales tax) to:

**Ascending View Publications**
**231 Crosby Drive**
**Indianapolis, IN 46227**

Please include your name, address, and phone number with your order.

**Free shipping on orders of more than 10 copies.**